VAN TIL & THE USE OF EVIDENCE

Thom Notaro

PRESBYTERIAN AND REFORMED PUBLISHING COMPANY
PHILLIPSBURG, NEW JERSEY 1980

ISBN: 0-87552-353-6

PRINTED IN THE UNITED STATES OF AMERICA

To Carol,
Evidence that
God loves me

Contents

Preface

THERE is a lot of confusion concerning the place of evidences in the apologetics of Cornelius Van Til. It does not seem to matter whether you have only begun to read his works or you have plowed through several of his major volumes on defending the faith. Nagging questions remain: Does Van Til rule out the use of evidences altogether? If so, what sort of dialogue is possible with non-Christians? If not, how can evidences be used in a presuppositional apologetic?

To some avowed Van Tilians such concerns are superfluous. Evidences are out of the question. All that matters is that the nonbeliever be told that his presuppositions conflict with biblical ones. It is that simple. The very notion of dialogue with non-Christians is suspect, according to this view, particularly if that dialogue relates to empirical facts. And it is an almost sure sign of faulty apologetic method if such discourse reaches any length, since presumably only a few points need to be made before a presuppositional standoff is achieved.

Both friends and foes of Dr. Van Til have commonly attributed this outlook to him. And perhaps that consensus is no more pronounced than in the mistaken assumption that Van Til allows no room for the use of evidences in defending Christianity.

I describe that assumption as *mistaken* because, as we shall see, Van Til has had a surprising amount of favorable things to say about evidences in his writings over the years. You may not be able to find them all in one discussion or under one cover—not even in his *Evidences* syllabus. And they are not as systematically presented as is his recurrent argument against the *misuse* of evidence. But they are there. And it is time Van Til be recognized for his appreciation of evidences as they are engaged in a presuppositional apologetic.

My primary aim in these pages is to gather the often-forgotten or unnoticed material Van Til has contributed on the proper use of evidence and to view it systematically. While this effort will involve some critique of his rivals, that is only incidental to the positive goal of seeing how evidences and presuppositions work together for Van Til. Only a few sample remarks from other authors are presented here as they help us focus on that issue.

Since I am trying to be faithful to Van Til's system, what I say here is not meant to be entirely new. The most original portions of this book are the discussion of the verification controversy (to which Van Til has not expressly spoken) and the examination of evidences pertaining to Jesus' resurrection described in five New Testament passages. Besides these, an effort has been made throughout to avoid simply parroting familiar

Van Tilian slogans. While paraphrasing some of his central themes, I hope to place old truths under new light so that some which may have been neglected would receive the attention they merit.

But I should stress that what I am seeking is an originality of *expression* and *application,* not an originality of commitment meant to contrast with Van Til's position. As far as I am concerned, the implications of his system are so rich and pervasive that there is no need to step outside the framework within which those implications arise. Perhaps this book will help to make explicit a few concerns implied in the works of the great Westminster apologist.

Anything like an exhaustive survey of types of Christian evidence is well beyond the scope of this little volume. And while it is not strictly an introduction to apologetics, those who have only dabbled in Van Tilian literature are encouraged to have a go at it. Technical language has been avoided where possible, the worst of which appears within the chapter on verifiability. On the other hand, readers familiar with Van Til's vocabulary, but still unclear concerning the role he gives to evidences, might find in the material gathered here the answers to their questions.

May we all become better defenders of the Christian faith.

PART I
Introductory Chapters

1

The Legitimacy of Evidences

MUCH debate has flourished in the arena of apologetics between those who stress the primacy of presuppositions and those who emphasize the empirical verifiability of Christianity. On the presuppositionalist side Cornelius Van Til and Gordon Clark are prominent names along with Rousas Rushdoony and Ronald Nash. Well-known figures identified as evidentialists include John Warwick Montgomery, J. Oliver Buswell, and Clark Pinnock. Many other names could receive mention here as siding more or less with one or the other position: E. J. Carnell, Gordon Lewis, Bernard Ramm, John Gerstner, Francis Schaeffer, and Norman Geisler are a few. Though some of these figures are difficult to categorize, their contributions generally lend support to either a presuppositionalist or an evidentialist persuasion.

With the line of opposition drawn between these two camps, it may seem odd to suggest that evidences play a legitimate role *within* presuppositional apologetics, specifically the apologetics of Cornelius Van Til. Has not Van Til repeatedly spurned the very idea of validating the claims of Scripture on the basis of what he calls "brute facts," facts whose meaning supposedly does not depend on God's revealed interpretation? If Dr. Van Til has made himself clear on any matter, is it not that the case for Christianity *cannot* rest on direct appeals to physical evidence either in past history or in our current experience? It would appear that evidences have no place in his system.

On the very first page of his *Apologetics* syllabus Van Til flatly declares, "It is impossible and useless to seek to vindicate Christianity as a historical religion by a discussion of facts only."[1] This sort of remark is typical of Dr. Van Til and can be found almost anywhere in his writings. His followers echo the same familiar refrain. Greg Bahnsen, for one, states, "The gospel . . . does not cater to rebellious man's demand for factual signs and logical argumentation that will pass the test of autonomous scrutiny."[2] Hear also Jim Halsey:

> The Christian can point to nothing outside the Bible for verification of the Bible because the simple fact is that everything outside the Bible derives its meaning from the interpretation given it by the Bible.[3]

These expressions are strongly reminiscent of Abraham Kuyper whose influence upon Van Til is well known. Kuyper had said,

---

[1] Cornelius Van Til, *Apologetics* (Syllabus, 1971), p. 1.

[2] Greg Bahnsen, "Apologetics," *Foundations of Christian Scholarship*, ed. Gary North (Vallecito, California: Ross House Books, 1976), p. 209.

[3] Jim S. Halsey, *For a Time Such As This: An Introduction to the Reformed Apologetic of Cornelius Van Til* (Philadelphia: Presbyterian and Reformed Publishing Co., 1976), p. 39.

When the Theologian stands in the presence of God, and God gives him some explanation of His existence as God, every idea of testing this self-communication of God by something else is absurd; hence, in the absence of such a touchstone, there can be no verification, and consequently no room for criticism.[4]

To those outside the presuppositionalist tradition, claims like these carry the ring of papal pronouncements and are about as arbitrary. For that reason many wonder how such edicts benefit the cause of Christian apologetics. Far from defending the faith, Van Til and company disdain evidence to the extent of defecting from the battle over the Bible's facticity—or at least that is the way some apologists see it. Clark Pinnock, for one, reads Van Til to say that "because [God] transcends the world, nothing in the world of factuality is capable of revealing him of itself."[5] With that in mind, Pinnock charges that Van Til "believes he can begin with God and Christianity without consulting objective reality."[6]

Pinnock is not alone in his interpretation. There is, of course, John Warwick Montgomery who complains that Van Til "eliminates all possibility of offering a positive demonstration of the truth of the Christian view."[7] And the verdict delivered by Gordon Lewis is that Van Til "has left the faith defenseless."[8]

---

[4]Abraham Kuyper, *Principles of Sacred Theology*, trans. by J. Hendrik De Vries (Grand Rapids: Wm. B. Eerdmans, 1954), p. 251.

[5]Clark H. Pinnock, "The Philosophy of Christian Evidences," *Jerusalem and Athens*, ed. E. R. Geehan (Philadelphia: Presbyterian and Reformed Publishing Co., 1971), p. 423.

[6]Ibid., p. 420.

[7]John Warwick Montgomery, "Once Upon an A Priori," ibid., p. 387.

[8]Gordon R. Lewis, "Van Til and Carnell," ibid., p. 361.

The quotations above from those both for and against Van Til all leave the impression that his system is very firmly anti-evidence. His opponents most expressly and with few exceptions have drawn that conclusion. So then, why speak as though evidences possess some kind of *legitimacy* within Van Til's apologetics? Has not that combination been ruled out by the very nature of the presuppositionalist versus evidentialist debate?

Contrary to what one might expect—especially if one commits the common fallacy of reading only segments of Van Til's works and extrapolating his whole system from a few passages—Van Til has more kind things to say about evidences and the use of reason than may at first meet the eye. An example can be found in the seventh and last summary point of his "My Credo":

> . . . we present the message and evidence for the Christian position as clearly as possible, knowing that because man is what the Christian says he is, the non-Christian will be able to understand in an intellectual sense the issues involved.[9]

In another place, we find Van Til supporting Benjamin Warfield's claim that "the Christian faith is not a blind faith but is faith based on evidence."[10] With Warfield and Charles Hodge he maintains that "Christianity meets every legitimate demand of reason" and "is not irrational" but "is capable of rational defense."[11]

---

[9]Van Til, "My Credo," ibid., p. 21.
[10]Van Til, *A Christian Theory of Knowledge* (Philadelphia: Presbyterian and Reformed Publishing Co., 1969), p. 250.
[11]Van Til, *Common Grace and the Gospel* (Philadelphia: Presbyterian and Reformed Publishing Co., 1972), p. 184.

If these statements sound uncharacteristic of Van Til, it is *not* because he has lapsed momentarily into a persuasion which conflicts with his better judgment and overall commitment. The fact is that Van Tilian apologetics reserves a significant place for evidence, for reason, and (most surprisingly) for theistic proof. As he himself put it, "I do not reject 'theistic proofs' but merely insist on formulating them in such a way as not to compromise the doctrines of Scripture."[12]

But how can this apparently pro-evidence, pro-reason, even pro-proof stance be harmonized with the seemingly anti-evidence posture viewed earlier? The answer to this question should begin to emerge on closer investigation of those earlier statements.

We first noted that Dr. Van Til saw no use or validity in apologetic discussions "of facts *only*."[13] The word "only" is an important qualifier implying that factual discussions are not absolutely ruled out but are proper when combined with other necessary considerations, namely, Christian presuppositions. Similar qualifiers appear in the statement we looked at from Greg Bahnsen: "The gospel does not cater to *rebellious* man's demand" for evidences and reasons "that will pass the test of *autonomous* scrutiny." Rather, as Van Til has noted, "Christianity meets every *legitimate* demand of reason."

---

[12]Van Til, *The Defense of the Faith* (Philadelphia: Presbyterian and Reformed Publishing Co., 1955, 1967), p. 197; *A Christian Theory of Knowledge*, p. 292.

[13]All italics in this and the following paragraph are my emphases added to quotations cited above.

The comment from Jim Halsey is a bit more difficult because the qualifying term is ambiguous: "The Christian can point to nothing *outside* the Bible for verification of the Bible." A possible problem is that "outside the Bible" can be construed at least two distinct ways.

In one sense, *nearly everything* man experiences is "outside the Bible." Most things are *physically* outside the pages of Scripture. It may sound as if none of these items (e.g., trees, stars, mountains, rain, human beings and the countless other objects in the created natural world) join in manifesting the truth of God. Indeed, that is what many regard Van Til to teach. But in another sense, *nothing* man experiences is "outside the Bible." Nothing in creation is outside the *authority* of Scripture.

It is in the second sense, and not the first, that Halsey's statement should be taken if it is to express Van Til's viewpoint. What Van Til denies is the existence of some sort of *autonomous* authority *independent* of Scripture. Were we to qualify the quotation by Kuyper according to Van Til's position, it would likewise read: ". . . in the absence of such [an autonomous] touchstone there can be no [independent] verification. . . ."[14]

Thus, a certain *kind* of verification is ruled out. But verification is not disqualified altogether. Inasmuch as

---

[14]Some warrant for these interpolations is provided by the context of Kuyper's statement. There he is discussing the "dependent character for Theology." Yet Kuyper did not himself make the qualifications I suggest here. And as we shall see in chapter 6, Van Til chose to differ with him specifically with regard to Kuyper's denial of *any* sort of theistic proof or verification.

all things come under the authority of Scripture, nothing is epistemologically or ethically outside the Bible. For that reason, the Christian *can* point to things physically or metaphysically outside the Bible for verification, as long as they are understood in accordance with Scripture's authority.[15] In other words, evidences can operate in keeping with what Van Til calls the "self-attestation" of Scripture. But that will be developed more fully later.

Perhaps this much has been established so far: that Van Til's presuppositionalism is not designed to forbid the discussion of facts, the use of reason, even the offering of proof or verification. To be sure, facts, reason, and proofs are very frequently misapplied in apologetics, and Van Til has shown tremendous concern over this problem. But his solution is not to exclude evidential considerations from presuppositional apologetics. He writes:

> I do not artificially separate induction from deduction, or reasoning about the facts of nature from reasoning in *a priori* analytical fashion about the nature of human-consciousness. On the contrary, I see induction and analytical reasoning as part of one process of interpretation.

This rather cryptic remark becomes clearer as one reads on:

> I would therefore engage in historical apologetics. (I do not personally do a great deal of this because my col-

---

[15] I incorporate the language of an epistemological/metaphysical distinction in order to suggest that the two senses of "outside the Bible" are closely related to Van Til's contrast between epistemological common ground and metaphysical common ground.

leagues in the other departments of the Seminary in which I teach are doing it better than I could do it.) Every bit of historical investigation . . . is bound to confirm the truth of the claims of the Christian position. But I would not talk endlessly about facts and more facts without ever challenging the non-believer's philosophy of fact.[16]

The two, therefore, must go together—induction and deduction, facts and the philosophy of facts, evidences and presuppositions.[17] Just as there may be a "legitimate demand of reason," there clearly is a legitimate place for evidences in Van Tilian apologetics. The following chapters will attempt to specify what that place is.

-----

[16]Van Til, *The Defense of the Faith*, p. 199.

[17]The name "evidentialist" as opposed to "presuppositionalist" is recognized as misleading when you see that there is no necessary conflict between Christian evidences and Christian presuppositions.

2

Evidences, Apologetics and Theology

DEBATES over the use of evidences characteristically reflect dissenting views concerning the definition of apologetics. It is generally accepted that the study of evidences belongs within the parameters of apologetics. What is not so readily agreed upon is the relationship of apologetics to systematic theology.

This is more than a merely academic controversy. If apologetics is not dependent on the findings of systematic theology, then the apologist is free to endorse an unspecified concept of God before moving on to urging belief in the God of Scripture. But will Scripture allow us to begin by defending no God in particular? Or must apologetics from the start confine itself to the defense of what the Bible teaches? Just how much overlap of systematics and apologetics is necessary?

The above question comes to bear specifically upon our understanding of evidences, since evidences fall within the boundary of apologetics. It asks, in effect, To what extent do evidences require a theological base? For an answer to this question we will focus attention briefly on the range and purpose of Christian apologetics. If the next few pages seem a bit tedious, have courage—they will help the rest of the book flow more easily.

According to Van Til, "Apologetics is the vindication of the Christian philosophy of life against the various forms of the non-Christian philosophy of life."[1] Inasmuch as apologetics examines philosophies of life it is a comprehensive concern. To be sure, apologetics aims more specifically at vindicating Christian *theism*. But Van Til sharply denies any illusion that theism can properly be considered without at least some attention being given to the other Christian doctrines. With Warfield, Van Til opposes the view that apologetics is concerned merely with "the *minimum* of Christianity." In Warfield's words, "What apologetics has to do with is certainly not any '*minimum*,' but just Christianity itself. . . ."[2]

Apologetics is an embracive discipline for Van Til because "Christian theism is a unit."[3] "We are not interested in discussing the existence of a God the nature of whom we do not know."[4] And as soon as we begin to elaborate upon God's nature, we enter into a discussion of other Christian doctrines—not only the doctrine of

---

[1]Van Til, *Apologetics*, p. 1.

[2]Benjamin B. Warfield, "Introductory Note," in Francis R. Beattie, *Apologetics*, Vol. I (Richmond: The Presbyterian Committee of Publication, 1903), p. 31.

[3]Van Til, *Apologetics*, p. 1.

[4]Ibid., p. 5.

God, but also the doctrines of man, Christ, salvation, the church, the last things, indeed all the foci of systematic theology.

If theism carries direct implications for all of theology, the apologetic task is really a defense of the whole system of Christianity, not just theism in its barest form. Thus conceived, apologetics becomes the shared concern of every theological department. It is not as though one department engages in a *formal* defense of the faith while the others deal with the *content* of biblical teaching. Van Til states it clearly, ". . . defense and positive statement go hand in hand."[5] All the various theological departments with their specific teachings are enlisted in the apologetic battle. Explains Van Til, "Every attack upon one of these is an attack upon the whole system of truth as we hold it."[6]

Thus, for Van Til, apologetics is an extremely broad concern, as broad as the entire field of theology. In turn, theology itself is by no means a narrow field of study. If God had addressed His revealed Word to only a small range or segment of man's experience, theology would then be limited accordingly. But to suggest that theology is a confined discipline alongside many diverse non-theological disciplines is to imply that God does not speak with authority to *all* of life. Are not even the studies of biology, psychology, history, and so on, governed by biblical principles and thereby extensions of theology? That seems to be Van Til's view: "The Bible is

---

[5]Ibid., p. 3.
[6]Van Til, *Christian-Theistic Evidences* (Syllabus, 1961), p. ii.

thought of as authoritative on everything of which it
speaks. Moreover, it speaks of everything . . . either directly or by implication."[7]

If theology entails man's application of Scripture to
every part of life, and the field of apologetics is as wide as
that of theology, then the apologetic arena spans all
experience and every discipline.[8] Like theology, apologetics draws attention to the manifold responsibilities
that grow out of God's authoritative revelation, responsibilities which touch every moment of human experience. In short, Christian apologetics has universal
dimensions. It concerns nothing less than a total world
view. That is why Van Til describes apologetics in terms
of a conflict between philosophies of life.

But what is it that distinguishes apologetics from the
study of theology? A helpful approach to this question
has been submitted by John Frame who currently teaches
apologetics at Westminster Seminary. He suggests that
apologetics and theology be viewed as distinct perspectives on the same body of truths. While both disciplines
involve the application of Scripture to all of life, the
distinct focus of apologetics is its application of Scripture

---

[7]Van Til, *Apologetics*, p. 2.

[8]My indebtedness to John Frame, Van Til's successor at Westminster
Seminary, would not be a very well kept secret. Here I accept his
definition of theology as the "application of God's word by persons to
all areas of life." While some may object to the notion of theology as
"application," I believe it is strictly in accordance with the Van Tilian
correlation between epistemology and ethics. The warrant for Frame's
definition will not be spelled out in this volume, though it is strongly
implied in later chapters regarding the covenantal framework for
knowledge.

to challenges and controversies. As theology, apologetics has everything to do with the doctrines of the faith. But as distinct from theology, it focuses on the *defense* of the faith. Again, defense and positive statement do not exclude each other. According to Frame, "The difference between the two [apologetics and systematic theology] in practice . . . becomes a *difference in emphasis* rather than of subject matter."[9]

In order to fill out the picture, it could be added parenthetically that Christian ethics and witnessing also provide distinct perspectives on theology and apologetics (not to mention Jay Adams's "nouthetic" counseling, which is Van Tilian to its core). Frame views ethics to be theology emphasizing man's *obligations*. I would add that ethics and apologetics overlap most explicitly in the area of elenctics, the study of man's moral obligation to believe.

As for witnessing, the focus is on the application of Scripture to Christian *character* lived before an unsaved world. In effect, witnessing is Christian character *on display*, exhibited in word and deed. The correlation between ethics and witnessing should be obvious: Christian character must develop in keeping with biblical obligations. But there may be some confusion over the relationship between apologetics and witnessing. Are the two related as pre-evangelism to evangelism, *á la* Clark Pinnock?[10] Not according to Van Til—he sees no

---

[9]John Frame, *Van Til: The Theologian* (Phillipsburg, N.J.: Pilgrim Publishing Co., 1976), p. 4.

[10]Pinnock, *Set Forth Your Case* (Nutley, N.J.: Craig Press, 1967), p. 8.

sharp distinction between witnessing and the defense of the faith.[11] As for the *distinction* between apologetics and witness, I am inclined to describe it as this: apologetics is something the Christian *does;* witness is something the Christian *is.*[12]

John Frame has coined the term "perspectivalism" to describe these various relations. The approach he has developed seems to provide an accurate picture of how Van Til views such closely knit concerns.

Summarizing what has been said so far in this chapter, I have noted that Van Til regards the defense of the faith to be inseparable from the presentation of scriptural dogma. Apologetics and theology are interdependent. This fact, coupled with Frame's emphasis on theology as application, gives both theology and apologetics an enormous range. But what is most important for this discussion is that the study of apologetics can at no point be extended beyond the governing principles of theology, not if it is rightly to be called *Christian* apologetics.

From what has preceded, it should be clear by now that, for Van Til, the study of evidences, as "a sub-

---

[11]Van Til, Response to Frederick R. Howe's "Kerygma and Apologia," *Jerusalem and Athens,* ed. E. R. Geehan (Philadelphia: Presbyterian and Reformed Publishing Co., 1971), p. 452.

[12]I do not suggest that *doing* is ruled out of witness. I believe, however, the primary focus is that one is *constituted* a witness. For example, in Acts 22:14, 15, Ananias says to Paul, "The God of our fathers has appointed you to know His will, and to see the Righteous One, and to hear an utterance from His mouth. For you will *be a witness* for Him to all men of what you have seen and heard." Do not Christ's words make a similar point in Matthew 4:19?: "Follow Me, and I will *make you* fishers of men." Note also Acts 1:8: ". . . and you shall *be* My witnesses. . . ."

division of apologetics," also requires a theological base.[13]

Those who are at odds with Dr. Van Til's position make every effort to disconnect apologetics and evidences from theology. Says John Warwick Montgomery, "Apologetics must never be confused with systematic theology. . . ."[14] Likewise, E. J. Carnell declares, "Statement and defense . . . are not the same thing. Statement draws on theology; defense draws on apologetics."[15] As we have seen, Pinnock restricts apologetics to the area of "pre-evangelism," while theology is reserved for the actual evangelistic task. And in a similar vein, "Apologetics and Christian evidences are not the gospel," says Bernard Ramm, "but if a man has a prejudice against the gospel it is the function of apologetics and evidences to remove that prejudice."[16]

Zealous as these men are to insulate evidences and apologetics from theology, Van Til would argue that theirs is a zeal not according to knowledge; no such division is possible. *Christian* evidences, like *Christian* apologetics, require a particular interpretation, namely, a Christian one.

It remains to be seen in what ways the study of evidences differs from the broader discipline of apologetics.

---

[13]Van Til, *Christian-Theistic Evidences*, p. i.

[14]Montgomery, "Once Upon an A Priori," p. 391.

[15]Edward John Carnell, *The Case for Orthodox Theology* (Philadelphia: The Westminster Press, 1959), p. 13, cited by Gordon R. Lewis, "Van Til and Carnell," p. 349.

[16]Bernard Ramm, *Protestant Christian Evidences* (Chicago: Moody Press, 1953, 1967), p. 15.

Again it is helpful to call upon John Frame's perspectival approach, which regards the two studies to be distinct in emphasis or focus. Both disciplines constitute the defense of the faith. But, as Van Til sees it, they are distinguished in that "evidences deals largely with the historical while apologetics deals largely with the philosophical aspect."[17] Elsewhere he submits this definition: "Christian-theistic evidences is . . . the defense of Christian theism against any attack that may be made upon it by 'science.'"[18] Here Van Til is using "science" in a wide sense. He adds that "in evidences it is primarily the factual question with which we deal."[19]

We may conclude from this that the study of Christian evidences, as understood by Van Til, is apologetics focusing on matters of fact. In other words, evidences is the application of Scripture to controversies primarily of a factual nature.

Now that we have seen the general relationship between evidences and these various disciplines, the remainder of this book will aim to show in more detail how evidences operate in presuppositional apologetics. Some specific questions which will require attention are these: In what sense are evidences "known" by non-Christians? What barriers must be overcome in order to come to an appreciation of the evidences? What exactly qualifies as evidence for the Christian faith? How does one *use* evidence in accordance with Dr. Van Til's system? The next two major sections deal with these and other closely related concerns.

---

[17]Van Til, *Apologetics*, p. 2.
[18]Van Til, *Christian-Theistic Evidences*, p. i.
[19]Ibid.

PART II
Knowledge and the Covenantal Framework

3

Two Senses of "Knowing"

THE study of evidences owes its complexity partly to the fact that there are two contrasting senses in which one may know the truth of God. When you read Van Til you find him saying time and again that depraved sinners *cannot know* or *understand* what is spiritually discerned. And yet, just as often it seems that Van Til is intensely concerned to point out that the unbeliever rebels precisely against what *is known* to him, that which he *understands* and cannot deny. Unless you realize that Van Til has in mind two senses of knowing, you can become very frustrated trying to sort out these two kinds of statements.

If there are two senses in which a person may know God's truth, that will have implications for the study of evidences. It will become necessary to ask in which way the facts are known and understood by sinners and whether such knowledge is of the sort that the apologist calls for men to embrace. We will need to consider what conditions must hold true in order for men to know and understand evidences in the manner required by Scripture.

Unless attention is given to these distinct ways of knowing, the knowledge we impart in the presentation of factual evidences may never live up to what the Bible demands.

What sort of distinction does Van Til draw between the two types of knowledge? As he sees it, the line of contrast is an ethical one. Man *"knows* God as Paul says so specifically in his letter to the Romans. . . . Yet ethically he does not know God."[1] Although knowledge is ordinarily considered a strictly epistemological concern, Van Til merges epistemology with ethics: ". . . by the sinner's epistemological reaction I mean his reaction as an ethically responsible creature of God."[2] Knowing is an ethical process.

A crucial underlying principle for Van Til is that man is a "covenant personality."[3] In the Bible a covenant is a binding contract issued by a sovereign to his subjects, involving obligations expressed in promises and solemn warnings. Ever since man was created he has owed undivided allegiance to his Creator. Man belongs to God. He is meant to be subject to the sovereign Lord. And the Lord has revealed to man the ethical requirements that would issue in life if obeyed, death if disobeyed.

Such obligations extend to all of behavior and thought so that all of man's life may be characterized as covenantal. In fact, man is personally confronted with the Lord of the covenant—His divine character and His holy will—in all

---

[1] Van Til, *A Christian Theory of Knowledge*, p. 245.
[2] Ibid., p. 293.
[3] Van Til, *Common Grace and the Gospel*, p. 69. See also Van Til, *The Defense of the Faith*, p. 152; *A Survey of Christian Epistemology* (Syllabus, 1932, 1969), p. 98.

of creation. As Van Til maintains, "God is man's ultimate environment. . . ."[4] The surrounding presence of God's person makes it impossible for man to take a "moral holiday." "Always and everywhere, in whatever he does and thinks as a scientist, philosopher, or theologian, whether learned or unlearned, man acts either as a covenant-keeper or a covenant-breaker."[5]

Van Til seems to have two ideas in mind when he includes knowledge under the heading of ethical or cove-nantal obligation to God. Obviously he wants to say that men ought to know God. They are responsible to acknowl-edge the existence of the Creator and Lord. But a second and far more complex idea is related to this first one. It is not only that men *ought* to know God. All men *do* know God. The problem is that sinners do not know God *as they ought*. That failure is not confined to "religious" knowledge—as if religion were a limited segment of one's life and thought. Sinners fail to know God as they ought in reference to all items of knowledge.

Knowing is therefore an ethical matter because all knowledge—all thought—entails obligation. "Every act of man's consciousness is moral in the most comprehen-sive sense of that term," says Van Til.[6] For Adam, "every fact was the bearer of a requirement."[7]

---

[4]Van Til, *The Defense of the Faith*, p. 42.

[5]Van Til, Response to Jack B. Rogers's "Van Til and Warfield on Scripture in the Westminster Confession," *Jerusalem and Athens*, ed. E. R. Geehan (Philadelphia: Presbyterian and Reformed Publishing Co., 1971), p. 167. See also Van Til, *Apologetics*, p. 26.

[6]Van Til, "Nature and Scripture," *The Infallible Word*, ed. Paul Woolley (Philadelphia: Presbyterian and Reformed Publishing Co., 1946), p. 274.

[7]Van Til, *Common Grace and the Gospel*, p. 72.

Facts reveal the will of God. The question of importance is whether man, in his thought life, accepts or rejects God's will. His knowledge either accords with divine requirements or it does not. It is characterized by either obedience or disobedience, submission or rebellion, wisdom or folly, spiritual discernment or ignorance. Man is a covenant-keeper whose knowledge honors God, or he is a covenant-breaker who knows, yet does not know as he ought. One way or the other, men do know God and are deeply responsible for what they know.

Van Til enumerates several specific items of knowledge of which even the remotest heathen is aware: for example, that God is the Creator of the world, that the world is controlled by God's providence, that the world manifests a certain nonsaving grace of God, that man is responsible for evil, that there is the need for God's special grace, and that man's failure to recognize God results in eternal punishment.[8]

On this matter Dr. Van Til sets himself clearly apart from most other apologists. They do not commonly hold the natural man accountable for actually possessing this much knowledge. In less specific terms than Van Til uses they will say, as Clark Pinnock says, that every man has certain "moral motions which he can no more eradicate than fly."[9] That is true. Or they may sound very much like Van Til when they explain that sinners willfully reject the otherwise clear evidence. Bernard Ramm, for example, comments that the problem of Christianity's truthfulness

---

[8]Van Til, *An Introduction to Systematic Theology* (Syllabus, 1971), pp. 79–80.

[9]Pinnock, *Set Forth Your Case*, p. 32.

is complicated by the "moral and spiritual disposition of the thinker."[10] Pinnock agrees that unbelief is "due to man's willful autonomy and refusal to bow before the living God."[11] And Paul Feinberg, a comrade of Montgomery, explains that "the difficulty is not with the evidence but with a rebellious will," and that "religious epistemology is related to human volition."[12]

These men will grant both that knowledge is in some sense an ethical matter and that certain conclusions persistently suggest themselves to the nonbeliever. But it would be out of character for a Pinnock or a Montgomery to list the items of knowledge that Van Til specifies the sinner indeed knows. As we have seen, these and other opponents to Van Til's method have denied the close connection between theology and apologetics. Hence, their defense of God is stated in much less explicit terms. Content first to talk about God in the most general categories, they seem reluctant to root the unbeliever's responsibility in the knowledge he actually holds concerning God's revealed character.

But as I have noted, Van Til's method is distinguished in that he affirms sinners do know the Creator God—the One who is holy, who is gracious, who controls the universe, who punishes the wicked. Along with Paul in Romans 1:20, Van Til reminds us often that God's "invisible attributes, His eternal power and divine nature, have

---

[10]Ramm, *Protestant Christian Evidences*, p. 250.

[11]Pinnock, *Set Forth Your Case*, p. 76.

[12]Paul D. Feinberg, "History: Public or Private? A Defense of John Warwick Montgomery's Philosophy of History," *Christian Scholar's Review*, 1, No. 4 (1971), 331.

been clearly seen, being understood through what has been made." And with David in Psalm 19:1, he sees the heavens telling of the "glory of God."

If all men are aware of the glory, the attributes, the eternal power and divine nature of God, as these verses plainly say, in what sense do *sinners* know and understand these things? They know in "an intellectual sense," says Van Til in "My Credo."[13] They have what he calls "theoretically correct" or "formally correct" knowledge about God.[14] "Granted that those who are covenant-breakers may in a restricted and limited sense see things for what they are," Van Til explains, "they see all these things, in the final sense, out of context."[15] In other words, while sinners know the truth of God, that knowledge isn't all that it should be. It is not knowledge embraced by the total man. It is knowledge cut away from its source and framework, emptied of its full significance and confined to a distorted intellectual realm.

By speaking of knowledge in an "intellectual sense," Van Til does not mean for a moment that knowledge can ever be an ethically neutral matter. The point is that the sinner will make every *effort* to evade the ethical implications of the facts. He will somehow attempt to hold the truth and, at the same time, suppress the covenantal significance of the truth. It is an impossible task and innumerable tensions arise.

The sinner is caught in an approach-avoidance conflict.

---

[13] Van Til, "My Credo," p. 21.
[14] Van Til, *The Defense of the Faith*, p. 17; *A Christian Theory of Knowledge*, p. 296.
[15] Van Til, *Christianity in Conflict*, II (Syllabus, 1962), 40.

Since he is the image of God, he is constantly reminded of his need of the One who created him. To deny God and His truth would be literal suicide. Man *needs* the truth, if only for his own survival. Yet at the same time the sinner will do anything to avoid the implications of the facts all around him. He is set against God's truth as a matter of principle. Thus he can neither avoid the truth nor accept it for what it is. Desperately he tries to accept the truth *for what it is not.* The result is that his whole life is an oscillation between the clearly revealed facts and his self-deluding fiction.

Knowledge in an "intellectual sense" contrasts with proper knowledge in that the former refuses to bow to the covenant Lord. Abraham Kuyper located the fundamental problem: ". . . you can receive no knowledge of God when you refuse to *receive* your knowledge of Him in absolute dependence upon Him."[16] Whereas the Christian's knowledge is self-consciously dependent, the non-Christian's knowledge pretends to be independent of God.

Knowledge in an "intellectual sense" lacks the fear of the Lord, which is the beginning of knowledge (Prov. 1:7). It fails to love God with all of the mind (Matt. 6:24). It does not honor God as God, or give thanks (Rom. 1:21). It is not the "full, accurate, living, or practical knowledge" that Charles Hodge notes Paul to equate with righteousness and holiness (Col. 3:10; Eph. 4:24).[17] And since it lacks all of these ingredients essential to genuine biblical knowledge, it is called "knowledge" in a provisional sense

---

[16]Kuyper, *Principles of Sacred Theology*, p. 252.

[17]Charles Hodge, *Systematic Theology*, II (Grand Rapids, Mich.: Wm. B. Eerdmans, 1973), 100, cited by Van Til, *A Defense of the Faith*, p. 75.

of the term, accenting the sinner's responsibility to love and submit to the Lord of truth. Ideally, ". . . what is meant by knowing God in Scripture is *knowing and loving* God," says Van Til; "this is *true* knowledge of God: the other is false."[18]

It should not be thought, however, that the sinner's knowledge is of no consequence. His knowledge leaves him "without excuse" (Rom. 1:20). And though such knowledge is a twisted fiction, like all fiction it must borrow heavily from fact. It is what Van Til commonly refers to as "borrowed capital."

Van Til does not at all deny that "the world may discover much truth without owning Christ as Truth."[19] But he calls such truth "borrowed" because it is lifted out of its proper context and emptied of its intended meaning.

Ideally, to know something is to know how it relates to other things—to know what it is for, where it is from, what obligations I have concerning it, what is its worth, what it signifies. The non-Christian scientist will give intellectual assent to all sorts of truth statements. But he will not be able to provide any ultimate explanation of the facts in terms of these relationships. The more explanation he gives, the more it will be seen that his interpretation runs counter to God's.

For example, as any scientist knows, apples come from trees and are normally good for eating. But where do apple trees come from? Ultimately the secular scientist will say that trees are a product of evolution, that is,

---

[18]Van Til, *A Defense of the Faith*, p. 17.
[19]Van Til, *The Case for Calvinism* (Philadelphia: Presbyterian and Reformed Publishing Co., 1964), p. 147.

chance. In other words, apple trees are not designed by God. Thus, for the nonbeliever, apples are Creator-denying apples: to really understand apples is to deny the biblical concept of God; apples *prove* that the God of Scripture does not exist, and each apple is an evidence *against* such a God. Ultimately, the nonexistence of God becomes part of the *definition* of apples.

Of course, the non-Christian rarely *states* the matter this strongly. He prefers to soften his expressions of rebellion against God in order to project an unbiased profile. At bottom, however, the stance of the nonbeliever is not unlike the portrayal I give it here. And as he is pressed to provide an ultimate interpretation of facts, he will voice increasingly explicit anti-Christian sentiments. Yes, even his definition of apples is affected because he defines *all* the terms of his experience on the basis of atheistic presuppositions.

According to the two senses of knowing, the nonbelieving scientist both knows and fails to know about apples. He has knowledge from God and of God, yet that knowledge is suppressed in ungodliness. He has truth, yet he holds that truth in untruth. What is evident about God is not accepted as evidence for God. Inventing an interpretation contrary to the significance God has implanted in the world, the sinner turns fact into fiction.

When Van Til says that sinners do not understand the deepest significance of any fact, he is talking about no minor difficulty. An apologist may be tempted to minimize this problematic; he may think he can go right ahead and build upon the sinner's partial knowledge. He forgets, though, that the sinner's knowledge is borrowed knowledge; it has been wrenched away from the only epistemological and ethical base upon which a Christian understanding can be built. Even the best building materials will collapse on a faulty foundation.

But does that mean the apologist may never appeal to the "theoretically" or "formally" correct ideas of the nonbeliever? Is there no point of contact between Christian and non-Christian thought?

Since man remains the image of God, the truth is not totally obliterated by sin. There *is* a point of contact, and appeals to borrowed knowledge can be effective—*under one condition:* The nonbeliever's borrowed knowledge can serve as building blocks of a genuine understanding only when his debased edifice of interpretation is abandoned in favor of the bedrock of Christian presuppositions. As the sinful structure is challenged and forsaken, borrowed truths are returned to their rightful place and significance. Only then does a man come to know God as he ought. "If there is no head-on collision with the systems of the natural man," writes Van Til, "there will be no point of contact with the sense of deity in the natural man."[20]

So without denying that sinners possess actual knowledge of God, Van Til insists that such an awareness represents no advance toward biblical knowledge if grounded in nonbiblical presuppositions. True knowledge is for the purpose of glorifying God. Any knowledge that disregards that end misses the mark completely. The glory of God is no secondary or optional matter.

---

[20]Van Til, *The Defense of the Faith*, p. 99.

Dr. Van Til has advanced a dual emphasis which few apologists have been willing to accept. He has said both that sinners have a wealth of knowledge about God and the world *and* that sinners know nothing as they ought. Plenty of apologists have noted that sinners possess some knowledge of a God and rebel against the truth. But few have recognized that rebellion as the great obstacle it is, as if the sinner's knowledge were merely incomplete.[21] Very few apologists are willing to follow Van Til's twofold stress to its fruition. They seem to think it will run them into an insoluble dilemma.

The fact of the matter is that Van Til's dual emphasis drives home a crucial apologetic point: since the God of Scripture has so clearly revealed to sinners His truth, and yet men strive to distort it beyond the point of recognition, man's problem of knowing therefore centers on his *rebellion against the covenant Lord.* The Christian apologist must confront men with the claims of that Lord.

At every moment God's natural revelation declares His glory to men. Yet the unbeliever wages perennial warfare by twisting each fact of that revelational flow as it comes to mind. He can never completely rid himself of the knowledge that continually arises. He can never step outside the covenantal context in which he was

---

[21]B. B. Warfield wrote in the "Introductory Note" to Beattie's *Apologetics*, p. 28, "Sinful and sinless men are, after all, both men; and being both men, are fundamentally alike and know fundamentally alike." See also Montgomery, "Once Upon an A Priori," p. 390: ". . . the Fall did not render Adam incapable of comprehending a word from God."

created. With the reminders of God's person surrounding him, he tries nevertheless to cast God out of remem-
brance.[22] But, as Van Til observes, "Deep down in his
mind every man knows that he is the creature of God
and responsible to God. Every man, at bottom, knows
that he is a covenant-breaker."[23]

---

[22]Van Til, *The Defense of the Faith*, p. 95.
[23]Van Til, *Apologetics*, p. 57.

4

What about
Epistemological Neutrality?

CHRISTIAN knowledge and non-Christian knowledge were sharply contrasted in the previous chapter. But there may still be a question whether it is possible for a sinner to suspend disbelief or adopt a neutral standpoint from which the claims of Scripture can be evaluated and then accepted or rejected.

A word from Clark Pinnock takes us to the heart of the issue: "The basis on which we rest our defense of the gospel consists of evidence open to *all* investigators."[1] That kind of statement is guaranteed to stir up fast and sometimes furious contention among apologists. A typically Van Tilian retort might be: "Yes, but are all investigators open to the evidence?" Pinnock's claim could easily be laid aside in such short order. But for our purposes a longer look would be worthwhile, because the topic of "openness" is central to the question of neutrality.

---

[1]Pinnock, *Set Forth Your Case*, p. 44.

Are the evidences "open to all investigators"? There are really two issues involved: one has to do with the openness of the investigator; the other has to do with the openness of the evidence. Van Til's followers have been quick to address themselves to the former issue by denying that sinful investigators are genuinely open. But they have not been nearly so prolific concerning the openness of evidences.

What do we mean by the openness of evidences? In the previous chapter Dr. Van Til was seen to have placed great stress on the fact that many things are known by sinful men, things that are clearly seen and evident to all. Van Til addresses such clarity under the heading of the "perspicuity of natural revelation."[2] His point is that the basic truths about God are *plain* facts, they are *obvious,* and the evidences are *open* to all men.

To be true to Van Til, one cannot very well deny the openness of the evidences. "Open," in this sense, means "apparent" or simply "evident." Only when "open" means "neutral" or "noncommittal" does Van Til reject the supposed openness of investigators. Pinnock's statement about "evidence open to all investigators" can be very confusing due to this ambiguity. Very clearly, what Van Til denies is "openness" in the sense of epistemological neutrality.

There may not seem to be anything distinctive about that denial. Do not all Christian apologists charge the sinner with prejudice against the truth? Who would

---

[2]Van Til, *Apologetics,* p. 34. See also p. 35 where Van Til speaks of the "objective perspicuity of nature."

allow that sinners are completely unbiased toward God's Word? No one who takes sin seriously.

Yet there is no difficulty lining up opponents to Van Til's view that certain Christian presuppositions are necessary in order for one to embrace the truth. We have seen that Clark Pinnock is one such adversary. Nevertheless, we find Pinnock now and then speaking out against "the myth of neutrality" and man's supposed "godlike objectivity."[3] One has to wonder how Pinnock, on the one hand, can deny the sinner's neutrality and yet, on the other hand, not favor Christian presuppositionalism as the remedy for the sinner's prejudice against God.

Perhaps Dr. Pinnock believes sinners are capable of a *provisional* neutrality—something less than absolute neutrality and godlike objectivity, yet not hopelessly subjective or biased. If nonbelievers are not as objective as they ought to be, maybe the apologist's job is precisely that—to urge sinners toward neutrality. Given that concept of apologetics, Pinnock is not likely to view presuppositionalism as the solution. It, *too*, falls short of genuine objectivity. Van Til's presuppositionalism, in particular, assumes Christianity "without consulting objective reality," says Pinnock.[4] To promote real objectivity, the apologist must shrewdly coax sinners into a somewhat neutral halfway house. And then, once this task of pre-evangelism has been accomplished, the nonbeliever is ready to assimilate the gospel without much resistance.

---

[3]Pinnock, *Set Forth Your Case*, p. 35.
[4]Pinnock, "The Philosophy of Christian Evidences," p. 420.

That, at least, is the way Pinnock and Ramm seem to view it. They, along with J. W. Montgomery, seem to believe that the case for Christianity can be brought before a neutral court. It is not that they say the sinner is unbiased. But they imply that the sinful person can first be reasoned into a more neutral frame of mind, whereupon he is friendlier toward the gospel. In this manner they stop short of requiring a complete overhaul of the sinner's epistemology. What they seem to allow is that the natural man is only relatively biased and confused, but that he can still arrive at a genuine understanding before coming all the way over to Christian presuppositions.

By the same token, Montgomery and others devalue presuppositions and place the maximum emphasis on presenting the facts themselves. If you argue that facts are meaningless without their proper interpretation, Montgomery's ready response is this: "The facts in themselves provide adequate criteria for choosing among variant interpretations of them."[5] So, for Montgomery, the facts speak for themselves.

Montgomery's motive is clear. He does not want to "naively assume the 'inspiration' or 'infallibility' of the New Testament records and then by circular reasoning attempt to prove what we have previously assumed." He intends to treat the New Testament "only as documents."[6]

---

[5]Montgomery, "Clark's Philosophy of History," *The Philosophy of Gordon H. Clark*, ed. Ronald Nash (Philadelphia: Presbyterian and Reformed Publishing Co.. 1968), p. 375.

[6]Montgomery, *History and Christianity* (Downers Grove: InterVarsity Press, 1964, 1965), p. 25.

A similar course had been taken by Benjamin Warfield many years earlier. He did not want to "found the whole Christian system upon the doctrine of plenary inspiration." Instead, the Scriptures must first be proven "authentic, historically credible, generally trustworthy, before we prove them inspired."[7] Warfield acknowledged that one must take his standpoint "not *above* the Scriptures, but *in* the Scriptures." Yet he added, ". . . surely he must first *have* Scripture, authenticated to him as such, before he can take his standpoint in them."[8]

Our understanding of the facts does not rely on prior theological commitments, according to this view. Presuppositions about the inspiration or infallibility of Scripture only beg the question, so it is argued. The facts must be allowed to decide the issue on their own merit. Dr. Ramm adds,

> If there are errors in Scripture or if there are no errors in Scripture is essentially a factual question, not a theological one. And therefore this issue is going to be settled eventually by empirical, factual studies and not by theological presuppositions.[9]

But is it true that the facts speak for themselves? What could Montgomery mean when he says the facts provide adequate criteria for their interpretation?

---

[7]Warfield, "The Real Problem of Inspiration," *The Inspiration and Authority of the Bible*, ed. Samuel G. Craig (Philadelphia: Presbyterian and Reformed Publishing Co., 1948), p. 210.

[8]Warfield, "Introductory Note," p. 24.

[9]Ramm, "The Relationship of Science, Factual Statements and the Doctrine of Biblical Inerrancy," *Journal of the American Scientific Affiliation*, 21, No. 4 (December, 1969), 102.

My sympathies lie with Ronald Nash who finds that to be a puzzling notion. Montgomery's view is too simplistic, says Nash. We do not merely "discover" the facts of history "out there," as Montgomery would lead us to believe. We "reconstruct" the past.[10] Nash explains, "There is no such thing as a fact apart from some interpretation and some imputed significance."[11] He offers this vivid illustration: A father takes his young son to a baseball game in which a player hits a timely home run. The father is ecstatic, whereas the son who is puzzled by all the excitement asks, "What happened?" Do both father and son witness the same fact?

A "yes and no" answer is possible. Both father and son are eyewitnesses. Each watches a hanging curveball travel from the pitcher to the batter and thence into the right field seats. But only the father perceives a home run. The son does not understand the rules of the game or the game's significance within the schedule. In order for the son to *re*-cognize the fact of a home run, he must first cognize the significance of the visual phenomena, integrating it into meaningful whole. Unless this takes place, the son may leave the ball park insisting he never saw a home run, even though he had witnessed the visual phenomena necessary for one.

The point of this illustration is expressed concisely by Van Til: "The human mind as the knowing subject makes its contribution to the knowledge it obtains."[12]

---

[10]Ronald H. Nash, "The Use and Abuse of History in Christian Apologetics," *Christian Scholar's Review*, 1, No. 3 (1971), 224.

[11]Ibid., p. 223.

[12]Van Til, *The Defense of the Faith*, p. 67.

Thus, if there is any sense in which facts speak for themselves, it is limited by the contribution of the knowing subject.

I would suggest there *is* a sense in which the facts themselves speak. If, with Van Til, we insist that there are no "brute facts," then all facts are significant because God made them to fit a particular interpretation. That is to say, all facts signify something. They signify God's truth. As Van Til comments, "For any fact to be a fact at all it must be a revelational fact."[13] That is the character of general revelation. The facts of the natural world, including man, do suggest a particular interpretation, namely, God's, and none other. We may even go so far as to say, with Van Til, that man's knowledge can be objective: "If the Christian position with respect to creation . . . is true, there is and must be objective knowledge."[14] Such objectivity, however, should not be confused with neutrality. Objective knowledge depends on God's prior interpretation of the objects.[15]

So, the facts do speak. They do have objective significance. But it is misleading to say without qualification that the facts provide criteria for their interpretation. To begin with, general revelation was never meant to be understood apart from special revelation. Even before the Fall, Adam and Eve received the two forms in conjunction. As Van Til notes, ". . . God's revelation in nature was from the outset of history meant to be taken

---

[13]Van Til, *Apologetics*, p. 36.
[14]Van Til, *The Defense of the Faith*, p. 43.
[15]Ibid.

conjointly with God's supernatural communication."[16]
You cannot disregard the one and still appreciate the
other for what it is.

Furthermore, since sin entered the world, our need for
special revelation is even greater. The presence of sin
has made the task of interpreting the facts much more
complex. As clear as general revelation may be, the
sinner, in his rebellion against the revealer of truth, will
not accept what the facts clearly signify. On the contrary,
the contribution that the nonbeliever makes to the
knowing process is not one that is amenable to what the
facts say.

It is not enough to say that the facts speak for themselves. True, the facts speak. But the sinner will not
listen.[17] Not only does the non-Christian fail to maintain a neutral outlook, but in doing so he subscribes to
an absolute autonomy in his epistemology. Van Til traces
the source of this error: "Facts and the truth about their
relationship to one another can be known by man, Satan
contended in effect, without getting any information
about them from God as their maker and controller."[18]

It is for this reason that Dr. Van Til, in contrast to his
critics, invariably turns the apologetic discussion back
to the matter of presuppositions. Though Pinnock and
others acknowledge the proclivity of sinners toward disbelief, they underestimate the controling effect of that

---

[16]Van Til, *Apologetics*, p. 34; See also Van Til, *Common Grace and
the Gospel*, p. 69.
[17]Van Til, *Apologetics*, p. 93.
[18]Ibid., p. 10.

sinful rebellion upon one's ability to perceive the factual evidences. Dr. Pinnock still seems to believe that the nonbeliever can arrive at some genuine understanding of the truth before giving in to Christian presuppositions.

But to those who hold such a view, Van Til offers this sobering warning: If we accommodate a supposedly neutral scientific method, ". . . we must allow that it is quite possible that at some future date all the miracles recorded in the Bible, not excluding the resurrection of Christ, may be explained by natural laws."[19]

At times apologists who are less than entirely sympathetic with Van Til can be found to echo his concern. In that manner Pinnock observes that "the fact of the resurrection is an undigestible surd for the naturalist."[20] Ramm likewise notes that for the naturalist, "the factuality of miracles is ruled out *a priori*. . . ."[21] He further explains that "every historiographer works with a formulated or assumed world view which governs completely what he admits as historical fact."[22] And he adds, ". . . any discussion of fact involves a doctrine of knowledge and theory of fact."[23]

Ramm's observations sound remarkably in tune with the Van Tilian theme. Nevertheless, something prevents Dr. Ramm from ascribing completely to Van Til's method. It is essentially the same barrier that stands between Pinnock and Van Til. For although Pinnock comments

---

[19]Van Til, *Christian-Theistic Evidences*, p. 65.
[20]Pinnock, *Set Forth Your Case*, p. 63.
[21]Ramm, *Protestant Christian Evidences*, p. 150.
[22]Ibid., p. 129.
[23]Ibid., p. 40.

that "psychologically there is no common ground between the Christian and non-Christian . . . ,"[24] both Pinnock and Ramm are willing to proceed as if some common *epistemological* ground remains intact. Their direct appeals to evidence—evidence that is not shaped by a Christian interpretation—imply that the unbelieving mind possesses at least a relative neutrality.

Such is the traditional view of apologetics. It was the view of no less a figure than Benjamin Warfield who maintained that "all minds are of the same essential structure. . . ."[25] But our look at the comparative functions of Christian and non-Christian minds suggested a different outlook. If to any extent we allow the legitimacy of the natural man's assumption of himself as an autonomous reference point for interpreting the facts, we cannot deny his right to twist the facts of Christianity at any point.[26] Autonomous man will not accept God's revelation in Scripture—that is agreed. But if we suspect there remains intact an element of neutrality in the non-Christian mind, Van Til adds, it is "no easier for sinners to accept God's revelation in nature. . . ."[27]

Without denying the clarity of the facts, and without

---

[24]Pinnock, *Set Forth Your Case*, p. 6. I understand the denial of "psychological" common ground to mean that sinners have a "gut" reaction against Christianity. The notion is conveniently vague, for it does not rule out a common epistemological ground—something Pinnock would not want to relinquish.

[25]Warfield, "Introductory Note," p. 30.

[26]Van Til, *The Defense of the Faith*, p. 93.

[27]Van Til, *Apologetics*, p. 36; See also Van Til, "Nature and Scripture," *The Infallible Word*, p. 280.

denying the legitimacy of evidences, it must not be thought that epistemological neutrality is possible for sinners. The facts must somehow be set within their proper theological framework for interpretation.

5

Evidence and Proof

THE two previous chapters have dealt with epistemological problems linked with covenantal rebellion. In chapter 3 it was seen that the sense in which a non-Christian knows the truth is characterized by dishonor toward God and is therefore directly opposite to Christian knowledge. In chapter 4 that opposition was seen to allow not even a provisional neutrality by which sinners can evaluate the biblical message.

In view of the nonbeliever's blindness to what the facts signify, it might seem as though evidences are not very useful after all—especially for Van Til. Many have suspected that all along. My purpose is to erase that false impression by showing what role evidences play within Van Til's system. But before doing so, something must be said regarding the impression that sinful rebellion renders evidences to be useless. This chapter will focus on the Van Tilian claim that the Christian system is capable of evidential proof.

As we have seen, the sinful orientation of autonomous

man results in what Van Til has called the "obscuration" of the facts.[1] Would not such obscuration make evidential argumentation a worthless enterprise? It is in this connection that Van Til's students sometimes conclude he reserves no place for rational or evidential appeals, much less proof.

But Dr. Van Til's own words should not go unnoticed on the matter: "This 'obscuration' in no wise subtracts from the fundamental perspicuity of God's revelation in nature."[2] In other words, the facts may be obscured and yet remain perspicuous to all. This is another way of saying that evidences may be open to the investigators even if the investigators are not open to the evidence. Perspicuity is an inherent characteristic of revelation. It does not depend on the disposition of the audience. For the same reason, the blindness of sinners does not lessen the fundamental clarity of God's revelation.

The conclusion Van Til draws from that premise will surprise some: "God's revelation is everywhere, and everywhere perspicuous. *Hence the theistic proofs are absolutely valid.*"[3]

To say that Van Til rejects theistic proofs altogether would be to miss his point. He writes, ". . . it is the difference between theistic proofs when rightly and when wrongly constructed that I have been anxious to stress."[4] Theistic proofs are valid "so far as they reflect

---

[1] Van Til, *An Introduction to Systematic Theology*, p. 79.
[2] Ibid.
[3] Van Til, *Common Grace and the Gospel*, p. 181, my emphasis.
[4] Ibid., p. 182.

the revelation of God."[5] Properly constructed, "they are but the restatement of the revelation of God. . . ."[6] Theistic proofs fail to convey the revelation of God when they are based on the assumption of man's autonomy.[7] What Van Til emphasizes is the "basic difference between a theistic proof that presupposes God and one that presupposes man as ultimate."[8]

Van Til is willing to speak of "true theistic proofs" taking the form of "ontological," "cosmological," and "teleological" proofs. Such proofs undertake to show, respectively, that the notions of existence, cause, and purpose are meaningless if they are not rooted in the existence of God.[9] Ultimately, the various forms of theistic proof may be reduced to one inclusive proof: ". . . that unless *this* God, the God of the Bible, the ultimate being, the Creator, the controller of the universe, be presupposed as the foundation of human experience, this experience operates in a void."[10]

So, in Christian theism there is "absolutely certain proof" for the existence of God. *Such* a God necessarily exists. Otherwise, says Van Til, "the uniformity of nature" and "the coherence of all things in the world" have no explanation.[11]

It is interesting that Van Til does not hesitate to allude to the uniformity and coherence of nature. These are notions of the sort that the sinner can no sooner do without and survive than stop breathing. That is not to

---

[5]Ibid.   [6]Ibid., p. 181.
[7]Ibid., p. 182.   [8]Ibid., p. 193.
[9]Ibid., p. 190.   [10]Ibid., p. 192.
[11]Van Til, *Apologetics*, pp. 64–65; *The Defense of the Faith*, p. 103.

say that nonbelievers accept a *Christian* conception of these terms. Sinners are set against a Christian understanding as a matter of principle. Yet in their practical day to day living, they must try to salvage some of the benefits of the Christian view—stripped of their covenantal obligations—or else all life would be chaotic.

Nonbelievers must not be allowed the luxury of mixing and matching biblical motifs with pagan premises. If a non-Christian rejects the biblical understanding of uniformity and coherence, he must face the desperate consequences. The true meaning and benefit of these terms is realized only when they are set in reference to the sovereign Lord of Scripture. Short of *such* an existing God, these rational inclinations must give way to the irrationality of a chance universe. In this sense, the uniformity and coherence of nature require the conclusion that God exists.

Along with this grand, universal proof, Van Til fully endorses Calvin's claim that man is presented with "innumerable proofs."[12] All the parts of creation offer unanimous and therefore inescapable evidence that Christianity is true. The range of proof is unmeasurable. Van Til cites, for one type of example, the Bible's majestic style and harmony, its fulfilled prophecies and its miracles, the words of Christ and His works, as objective demonstrations of Scripture's divinity.[13]

Van Til finds proof not only in special revelation,

---

[12]Van Til, *The Defense of the Faith,* p. 152, citing John Calvin's *Institutes,* Bk. I, Chap. V, Sec. 2.
[13]Van Til, *A Christian Theory of Knowledge,* p. 228.

but in every fact of general revelation. On this point he could hardly be more explicit:

> . . . surely the Reformed believer should stress with Calvin that *every* fact of history, here and now actually is a revelation of God. Hence *any* fact and *every* fact proves the evidence of God and therefore the truth of Scriptures. If this is not the case, *no* fact *ever* will.[14]

Traditionally, the study of evidences has centered attention on the unusual features of Christianity—odd phenomena which defy naturalistic explanation. As would be expected, miracles such as the parting of waters, the feeding of thousands, and the raising of the dead have received frequent mention along with the amazing growth of the church and preservation of the biblical text. Certainly, Dr. Van Til does not disqualify such types of evidences. They serve as proof when viewed within their proper framework. But the uniqueness of Van Til's system is highlighted by his claim that *all* facts are revelational. It is not only a selected body of unusual phenomena that defies naturalistic explanation. *All* facts, whether natural or supernatural, defy naturalistic explanation. Every fact signifies that it is controlled *by God*.[15] Otherwise, it signifies nothing. Either God is proven by every fact or we are left with meaninglessness.

The implications of this point should be clear. We are now able to answer the question as to what qualifies as

---

[14]Van Til, *An Introduction to Systematic Theology*, p. 17, Van Til's emphases! See also, Van Til, *Common Grace and the Gospel*, p. 72; *Apologetics*, p. 36.
[15]Van Til, *The Defense of the Faith*, p. 195.

evidence. For Van Til, *everything* is evidence—every fact, every object, every event properly understood is evidence for Christianity. Furthermore, every bit of evidence, as he sees it, *proves with absolute validity* the truth of God's Word.

Here again, Van Til is to be contrasted with other apologists. Typically, they have retold the maxims of J. Gresham Machen or B. B. Warfield (both of whom Van Til highly respected in all other regards), to the effect that probability is the best the evidence can do;[16] or as Clark Pinnock would vouchsafe, ". . . a probable argument is better than an improbable one."[17] They have resigned themselves to presenting evidence which is only probable, and which, in the words of Warfield, "leaves open the metaphysical possibility of its being mistaken."[18]

But from Van Til's outlook, it is they who have underestimated the weight of the evidence. They have not given the evidence credit for carrying absolute proof. In effect, they have inadvertently implied that God has not clearly revealed Himself in nature.

There appears to be a big difference in the way Van Til and his opponents define "proof." When Van Til speaks

---

[16]J. Gresham Machen, "History and Faith," *Christianity Today* 8, No. 24 (September 11, 1964), 26; Warfield, "The Real Problem of Inspiration," p. 218.

[17]Pinnock, "The Philosophy of Christian Evidences," p. 423. See also *Set Forth Your Case*, p. 45.

[18]Warfield, "The Real Problem of Inspiration," p. 218. When Warfield speaks of the possibility of the evidence being "mistaken," it is not clear to me whether he means that it may be in *error* or simply that it may be *misunderstood* by the listener.

of proof, he is talking about the objective revelation, regardless of whether man believes or not. Others, however, seem to view proof as contingent upon belief; hence, to prove is to convince.

Surely Van Til would not deny that theistic proof is capable of inducing belief. For those regenerated by the Holy Spirit, proof does convince. But that differs from saying that proof exists *only* when men are convinced.

Those who hold the latter view would have to say that the proof offered by the apologist is relative to the listener's response and therefore not absolute—not all men become believers. Without *strict* proof available, the argument for Christianity is only probable. Warfield seems to take this position. The way he explains it, the sinner's ability to "mistake" the evidence is linked directly to the fact that the argument is not strictly demonstrative.[19] Disbelief is traceable in part to the mere probability of the case.

There is one sense in which we might concede that absolute proof is beyond the ability of the apologist. Perhaps it should be granted that human fallibility prohibits him from *formulating* and *representing* the available proof in all its certainty. But such a lack of cogency would be traceable to the apologist's presentation. It would not mean that the evidence itself fails to constitute absolute proof, as some maintain.

When Warfield advocates a probability argument, it is not clear whether he thinks the *evidence* is somehow

_____

[19]Ibid.

inconclusive or whether the problem is simply in the *apologist's treatment* of the evidence. Perhaps Warfield did not draw that distinction. For whatever reason, he did not acknowledge the availability of absolute proof.

Van Til does: "The argument may be poorly stated, and may never be adequately stated. But in itself the argument is absolutely sound."[20] Disbelief or "obscuration" of the facts does not detract from the clarity or weight of the evidence. For Van Til proof is not what men uniformly believe but what men *ought* uniformly to believe.

So it is not just any notion of proof that Van Til supports. Surely he does not condone such proofs as would compromise biblical doctrines. And he clearly opposes those that imply sinners somehow maintain an excuse for disbelief. As Van Til often laments, the theistic proofs have traditionally committed these errors. They have implied that sinners are not fully to blame for their ignorance. They have allowed that God can be properly known before one is willing to submit to His authority. They have been content to prove *a* god who or which is other than *the* God who has presented Himself in Scripture. But inasmuch as no god other than the true God exists, the traditional theistic proofs have proved nothing.

The proof Van Til condones is proof that operates in full conformity with the biblical notion of God. It is proof that recognizes the evidences for what God has

---

[20]Van Til, *A Christian Theory of Knowledge*, p. 291.

made them. And when seen within the framework of God as the covenantal Lord over all the facts, that evidence is appreciated to constitute nothing less than absolutely valid proof for the Christian system.

PART III
Presuppositional Verification

6

A Close-Up of Verifiability

THE main thrust of the previous chapter should be clear: Dr. Van Til condones a particular sort of theistic proof. I admit to introducing a flood of quotations to that effect. Yet more support could have been cited.[1] The frequency with which Van Til defends the notion of proof is alarming compared to what one might expect.

If Van Til reserves room for theistic proof, would he also endorse a type of *verifiability?* According to one of his advocates, Charles Horne, Van Til "rejects all efforts at verification."[2] That verdict seems to find support in

---

[1]In addition to the passages I cited, John Frame in *Van Til: The Theologian*, p. 9 cites Van Til, *An Introduction to Systematic Theology*, pp. 102ff., 196; *The Defense of the Faith*, p. 196; *A Christian Theory of Knowledge*, p. 292.

[2]Charles M. Horne, "Van Til and Carnell," *Jerusalem and Athens*, ed. E. R. Geehan (Philadelphia: Presbyterian and Reformed Publishing Co., 1971), p. 379.

the fact that Abraham Kuyper, a forerunner to Van Til, disapproved of verification straightforwardly.[3]

Yet it is important to remember that Van Til does not follow Kuyper's lead uncritically. As Van Til sees it, Kuyper rightly "stressed the natural man's ethical alienation from God . . ." but drew "the illegitimate conclusion that the natural man is unable to understand the intellectual argument for Christianity in any sense."[4] In Kuyper's own words: "Let it not be said, that an infinite number of things are manifest and knowable of God, in the works of creation, in history, and in the experiences of our own inner life. . . ."[5]

Unlike Van Til, Kuyper did not differentiate the two senses of knowing. He did not allow that natural revelation is somehow clearly seen by sinners.[6] He regarded rational defense of the faith to be useless and therefore virtually rejected the study of apologetics,[7] although he practiced apologetics in spite of his playing it down.[8]

Van Til, in contrast to Kuyper, affirms that natural revelation provides proof—proof that does not pretend to be autonomous, but proof that does justice to scriptural teachings. What would keep Van Til from endorsing a type of verifiability that would meet these same conditions? Is verification not another way of talking

---

[3]Kuyper, *Principles of Sacred Theology*, p. 251.
[4]Van Til, *A Christian Theory of Knowledge*, p. 246.
[5]Kuyper, *Principles of Sacred Theology*, p. 250.
[6]Van Til, *A Christian Theory of Knowledge*, pp. 230ff.
[7]Ibid., p. 234.
[8]Ibid., p. 253.

about proof?[9] Of course, both proof and verification can be fallaciously constructed. But when these accord with Scripture, Van Til's method excludes neither.

Not that Dr. Van Til has explicitly condoned the notion of biblical verifiability—he has not discussed that term in writing, as far as I know. And some have criticized him heavily for not addressing the verification controversy, which grew out of recent analytic philosophy. Clark Pinnock, for one, indicts Van Til for "tragic irrelevance" at a time when philosophers are asking for verification of ultimate claims.[10]

But just because Van Til has not spoken directly to that philosophic tradition, that in no way indicates that his contributions are irrelevant to that issue. There are many topics to which Van Tilian principles have not been applied explicitly, yet to which they are deeply relevant. Van Til has always been concerned with a biblical world view, and the implications of his thought are only beginning to be extended to a wide range of fields and topics under that embracive concern.

Van Til's apologetic is loaded with repercussions for the verification controversy. A look at recent developments in the notion of verifiability will help to illustrate this point.

The verification controversy originally focused on the question raised by logical positivists in the 1920s as

---

[9]As I note below, the meaning of "verification" has undergone several stages of metamorphosis in the history of analytic philosophy. I am content to use the term less technically as a synonym of "proof," subject to the qualifications assigned by Van Til to that term.

[10]Pinnock, "The Philosophy of Christian Evidences," p. 424.

to whether religious and metaphysical language are meaningful. For example, does language about *God, angels, heaven,* and *hell* or *being, substance,* and *causality* say anything about the facts of our experience? Do such terms refer to anything we can experience with our five senses and thus verify? If not, what difference does such talk make in the world we can *observe?* Would we not be better off if we rid our language of these non-*sense* expressions?

Early positivists did just that. With remarkable ease they dismissed theological language from the domain of the factually significant. Since God could not be directly observed (seen, touched, heard, smelled, tasted), language about Him failed the test of verifiability. It was considered cognitively meaningless.

There were high expectations of the early verifiability criterion. It would give the edifice of philosophy a long-overdue house cleaning. Speculative notions, which once cluttered rooms of thought, could be put out as if for trash collection. Philosophers and scientists could abide together in peaceful harmony as long as unverifiable speculations did not intrude and bog down communication.

But before long, the dream house was divided against itself. First, the verifiability criterion could not pass its own test—it could not be verified. Second, the criterion was geared only toward testing *statements* but did not give adequate account of the meaningfulness of other types of sentences such as questions, requests, and expressions of attitude or emotion. Third, the criterion originally required *conclusive* verifiability of assertions. But conclusive verifiability not only eliminated theology and metaphysics: it threatened to do away with the very sort of scientific findings its inventors sought to protect. The criterion was modified so that it required observations that would "count for or against" a statement though not conclusively so. Fourth, the early criterion naively treated observation as a simple, straightforward task. But the inevitable question surfaced with disturbing frequency: what qualifies as an observation counting for or against a statement?

The question persists. And it leaves the original criterion far behind. While Antony Flew was announcing that theological language died "the death of a thousand qualifications,"[11] the bell was tolling ever so loudly for the verifiability criterion itself and its counterpart in falsifiability.

Although analytic philosophers have not, as a whole, repented in sackcloth and ashes, they have more recently acknowledged that verification by observation is often a very complex process. The line between observation language and nonobservation language is not as clear-cut as it was once thought to be. That makes it much more difficult to decide what kinds of language are verifiable and what are not. If we grant that God is not *directly* observable, could he not yet be *indirectly* observable, and thus have everything to do with the facts of our experience?

In 1964 language philosopher William Alston gave expression to an increasingly popular reply to that sort

---

[11]Antony Flew, "Theology and Falsification," *New Essays In Philosophical Theology,* ed. Flew and Alasdair MacIntyre (London: SCM Press, 1955), p. 96.

of question.[12] He suggested that "no nonobservation statement logically implies any observation statement by itself, but only in conjunction with other statements."[13] Alston provides this illustration:

> Ernie Smith has intense unconscious hostility toward his father.

is considered a nonobservational statement (assuming Ernie never displayed such hostility directly toward his father). That nonobservational statement would not necessarily imply the observation,

> Ernie Smith flared up at Mr. Jones.

The lone fact that such a flare-up at Mr. Jones occurred would not "count for" the existence of unconscious hostility toward Mr. Smith. But Alston offers additional conditions providing a link between the supposedly nonobservational statement and the clearly observational one:

> Mr. Jones looks enough like Ernie's father to permit a displacement of the hostility onto him.
>
> The repression is not so severe as to permit no expression.
>
> The hostility has not all been worked off in other ways.

Given these and other relevant premises, Ernie's flare-up at Mr. Jones can now be interpreted as observable evidence for his hostility toward his father.

We could draw up an example using theological

---

[12]William P. Alston, "Empiricist Criteria of Meaningfulness," *Philosophy of Language* (Englewood Cliffs, N.J.: Prentice-Hall, 1964), pp. 62–83.

[13]Ibid., p. 77.

language to give us a hint as to how Alston's idea of confirmability might work for Christian evidences:

> God is love.

is considered by many to be a nonobservational statement. And most would deny that the observation,

> It rained in Philadelphia last night.

would "count for" the assertion that God is love. But what if we introduce additional premises?:

> God is the controller of nature.
>
> Men deserve no blessings from God.
>
> Rain is a blessing resulting from the love of God in Christ.
>
> God sends rain on the righteous and the unrighteous.
>
> Philadelphia is populated by both righteous and unrighteous people.

These additional premises form a system of understanding wherein rain in Philadelphia is observed as evidence for the love of God.

As Alston explains, "The presence or absence of a given piece of data counts not just for or against one particular hypothesis, but rather for or against the whole body of premises used in deriving it."[14] In other words, statements receive verification or (as Alston prefers) confirmation not simply by direct ties with observable facts: a whole system of interwoven premises determines whether so-called nonobservation statements correspond with the factual state of affairs.

---

[14]Ibid.

What Alston describes has *formal* similarities with what Van Til has said all along, in different terms. While Alston says that a *hypothesis* is derived from a *body* of *premises*, Van Til stresses that Christian theistic *presuppositions* are rooted in a unified *system* of *doctrines*.[15] Where Alston speaks of *data* or *observations* counting for a hypothesis in conjunction with premises, Van Til speaks of *facts* or *evidences* proving God's truth as a system.[16] And like Alston, Van Til emphasizes the need for "indirect" appeals to evidence "rather than direct" appeals.[17]

Alston is no Van Tilian. But he has adopted a much more realistic notion of observation and confirmation than the old verifiability criterion of the positivists. It is remarkable how many parallels there are between Alston's argument and Van Til's. Among other things, it shows that Van Til's apologetic is *not* irrelevant to recent discussions of verifiability.

One likely point of difference between Van Til and Alston would be on the distinction between observational and nonobservational statements. While Alston regards additional premises to mediate between the two types of language, he does not seem to challenge the distinction itself. It is hard to imagine, on the other hand, that Van Til would be satisfied to call theological language nonobservational—at least in any strict sense. Though "no man has seen God at any time" (John

---

[15]Van Til, *The Defense of the Faith*, pp. 114–15.
[16]Van Til, *Apologetics*, p. 97: ". . . any individual fact of this system is what it is primarily because of its relation to this system."
[17]Van Til, *The Defense of the Faith*, p. 100.

1:18), Van Til reminds us that "His invisible attributes . . . have been clearly seen" (Rom. 1:20); likewise, "The heavens are telling of the glory of God; and the firmament is declaring the work of His hands," even though "There is no speech, nor are there words; their voice is not heard" (Ps. 19:1, 3). Though God may not be directly observed, He has *revealed* Himself. His revelation is perspicuous. Thus, theological language is always observational in some sense.

An analytic philosopher who does challenge the distinction between observational and nonobservational language is Willard Quine. Specifically, Quine is dissatisfied with the familiar distinction between synthetic and analytic propositions. A rigid distinction between these is responsible for what Quine calls the "radical reductionism" of early verificationists.[18] In other words, Quine opposes the assumption that the factual or observational element of language could operate independently of the definitional element.

Within any system, explains Quine, some commitments are more central than others.[19] Those that are more central have a defining or controling effect upon the rest. Those more peripheral are more readily altered by experience. The former are less observational and the latter are more observational. But the difference is one of degree. All commitments within the system must somehow answer to experience and are thus more or less observational. At the same time all commitments take

---

[18]Willard Van Orman Quine, *From a Logical Point of View* (Cambridge, Massachusetts: Harvard University Press, 1953, 1964), p. 38.
[19]Ibid., p. 42ff.

on a definitional character as part of the system and are thus only relatively affected by observations. Generally speaking, it is the system as a whole that is confirmed or disconfirmed by experience.

So, both Quine and Alston see the verifiability criterion to be too simplistic. They both emphasize the systematic character of language. And both propose an indirect method of confirming statements which takes into account the function of systems in understanding experience. But Quine, even more than Alston, parallels Van Til on the relative interplay between central commitments (or presuppositions) and peripheral ones (or factual evidences). For Van Til, the reciprocal relationship between the two is what he endorses in the method of circular argument.[20]

As we noted earlier, Van Til refuses to separate analytic argument from factual argument but sees them as one process.[21] The facts and their proper interpretation within the Christian system of doctrines form a unit, and "every attack upon one of these is an attack upon the whole system of truth as we hold it."[22] It is according to this interdependence that non-Christian systems are disconfirmed by their inability to account for the facts.[23]

The similarities Alston, Quine, and other language analysts show with Van Til are wholly unintentional.

---

[20]Van Til, *Apologetics*, p. 62; *The Defense of the Faith*, p. 101.

[21]Van Til, *The Defense of the Faith*, p. 199: "I do not artificially separate induction from deduction, or reasoning about the facts of nature from reasoning in *a priori* analytical fashion. . . ."

[22]Van Til, *Christian-Theistic Evidences*, p. ii.

[23]Van Til, *Common Grace and the Gospel*, p. 192.

They represent a positive development in recent philosophy which may be characterized by the Van Tilian term "borrowed capital."[24] To that extent they help us to understand the possibilities for composing genuine proof or verification of the Christian system, using the wealth of evidences available.

While Dr. Van Til has not interacted explicitly with the verification controversy, John Frame has. As one who is both an ardent disciple of Van Til and a knowledgeable student of analytic philosophy, Frame heartily applauds a particular notion of biblical verifiability.[25] According to Frame, religious language is verifiable because it is ordinary language.[26] Among other things, this "ordinariness" has to do with the fact that God's truth is revealed to us in the immanent field of our experience (for example, the natural world, the pages of Scripture), and that God's revelation has bearing upon the facts of our situation.

At the same time, Frame notes, religious language is odd language—it states basic convictions which tend

---

[24]Another non-Christian whose contribution should not go unmentioned in this regard is Thomas Kuhn, *The Structure of Scientific Revolutions* (Chicago: University of Chicago Press, 1962). Kuhn accents the role conceptual models play in our interpretation of data. He points out that scientific revolutions occur not so much because of the discovery of new data, but because scientists choose to interpret familiar data according to unprecedented models.

[25]Frame, "God and Biblical Language: Transcendence and Immanence," *God's Inerrant Word*, ed. John Warwick Montgomery (Minneapolis, MN: Bethany Fellowship, 1974), p. 166.

[26]Ibid.

to sidestep verification; it transcends the world of experience.[27]

Thus, biblical language is both ordinary and odd, immanent and transcendent, observational yet not directly so; it can be known truly but not exhaustively; it interprets the facts yet is proven by the facts; it is verifiable but not falsifiable.[28]

Frame notes that when verificationists have opposed the facticity of religious language they have limited their attention to the "oddness" of such language. But he comments, "If an analysis of religious language is to be adequate, it must take *both* features into account, not just one of them."[29] The two, after all, are dual features of one systematic language. They are not two types of language competing with each other. Nor must we choose one or the other. We are left neither with Barth's "Wholly Other," which is beyond the ordinary world of experience, nor with a god who can be explained

---

[27]Ibid., pp. 166–67, 173.

[28]That is to say, Christianity can never be proven false. There is a sense in which biblical claims could be called "hypothetically falsifiable." That only means that if certain conditions obtained (or failed to), Christianity would not be true. Paul writes, for example, ". . . *if* Christ has not been raised, your faith is worthless" (I Cor. 15:17). Or consider a typically Van Tilian manner of speaking: *if* the God of Scripture were not the Creator and Controller of the universe, human experience would be void of meaning. "Hypothetical falsifiability" simply draws attention to the interdependence of doctrines. And because of the ultimate coherence of the Christian system, it says in effect, "if the biblical message were not true, it would be false." Such "falsifiability" is therefore harmless—the hypotheses can never be granted. And Christianity is never *really* falsifiable.

[29]Frame, "God and Biblical Language: Transcendence and Immanence," p. 166.

exhaustively in immanentistic, scientific terms. The "oddness" and "ordinariness" of religious language are correlative features. They speak of the intricate reciprocity between transcendent norms and immanent facts. The two features are engaged in a circular interplay between Christian presuppositions and Christian evidences.

The apparent parallels between Frame and Alston or Quine need not be spelled out. Most important is Frame's willingness to follow Van Til where neither Alston nor Quine would dare go. For notwithstanding the formal resemblance the latter bear with Van Til's method, they are very much unlike him in this crucial respect: Dr. Van Til, and Frame with him, follows the biblical teaching that language (indeed, all of life) is ethically qualified. Men are obligated to adopt and express certain basic commitments and not others. They are obligated to believe and obey the truth of God, which is made evident in revelation. No other system is evident, and there is no excuse for holding other views.

By direct inference, it must be concluded not only that Christianity is verifiable, but that it is *conclusively* so. All the facts declare the glory of God, or they say nothing at all.

Quine and Alston have deliberately substituted confirmability for what they thought was an overly ambitious claim to conclusive verifiability. And they were right in one respect: empirical observations alone can offer no absolute certainty. But as Van Til would indicate, not even a probable confirmability can be achieved without a Christian system of understanding. Truth claims are verifiable on one basis only, and that basis is the framework of Christian-theistic presuppositions.

7

Presenting
Presuppositional Evidences

WHETHER we call it "proof" or "verification" or simply "presenting the evidence,"
the method Van Til insists on is an indirect
one rather than a direct one. An indirect approach
accounts for the importance of Christian presuppositions in the interpretation of evidence. A direct one does
not; it attempts to introduce evidences without placing
them in a biblical framework. The problem is that apart
from a biblical framework, so-called "evidences" do not
really evidence what they are meant to. And sinners as a
matter of course impose on experience an interpretation
foreign to what the evidences properly signify. Vainly
the unbeliever tries to grasp onto truths while emptying
those truths of their God-given implications. It is an
endless task. Revelation continues to make known the
existence and character of God, but just as continually
the sinful mind is at work producing its own account of
what the facts say.

Though sinful rebellion is a continual process, it is
not always flagrant from our human point of view.

Non-Christians are often amiable. They may demonstrate relatively good behavior.[1] They may even assent to the existence of a god or the idea of Jesus' resurrection. But Van Til warns us not to think that a formal assent to these ideas brings a person any closer to a genuine understanding. Non-Christians do not rule out "the strange and the weird."[2] A resurrection from the dead is just the sort of thing people are amused to find in Ripley's *Believe It or Not*,[3] not to mention the recent cinema. As Van Til explains, the natural man "need not hesitate, on his principles, to accept the *fact* of the resurrection at all. But for him that fact is a different sort of fact from what it is for the Christian. It is not the same fact at all."[4]

In the same way, nonbelievers may admit some idea of creation but reject biblical teaching by "substituting another meaning for the word creation."[5] The pattern extends to all the Christian doctrines. As a result, says Van Til, the Christian apologist "cannot find a direct point of contact in any of the accepted concepts of the natural man."[6] This applies not only to "religious" concepts but also to such notions as atoms and the laws of gravitation[7]—indeed all facts are redefined to mean something other than what they truly are.[8]

---

[1] Van Til, *The Defense of the Faith*, p. 50.
[2] Van Til, *Christian-Theistic Evidences*, p. 97.
[3] Van Til, *The Defense of the Faith*, p. 240.
[4] Van Til, *Apologetics*, p. 95.
[5] Van Til, *Christian-Theistic Evidences*, p. 93.
[6] Van Til, *The Defense of the Faith*, p. 112.
[7] Van Til, *An Introduction to Systematic Theology*, p. 26.
[8] Van Til, *The Defense of the Faith*, p. 172.

It is as if the sinner tries to create a new *world*. When he looks at the world around him, he sees the revelation of God everywhere, but he imputes to the world an interpretation of his own contrivance. It is an understatement to say that sinners twist the facts—sinners flatly deny the facts. They may use the same language as do Christians; they may even manifest similar patterns of behavior. But eventually this parallel breaks down. The similarity extends only as far as the non-Christian is inconsistent with his anti-biblical principles.[9] If he were consistent, no communication would be possible between believer and nonbeliever. Since man is the image of God, he can never completely sever himself from some semblance of the truth which is formally, intellectually, or theoretically correct. But ultimately the sinner prefers to talk about a different set of "facts," which is to say, he prefers a fiction.

There are no facts other than God's facts. To substitute any other interpretation of the world for God's interpretation is to "exchange the truth of God for a lie" (Rom. 1:25). Nevertheless, it is what sinners do with a vengeance: instead of knowledge of God, they prefer futile speculations; in place of the natural, they desire the unnatural; rather than accept God's will, they pursue vanity.

That is why appeals to evidence cannot be direct. Such appeals would count for nothing. Implicitly they would approve the sinner's method of interpreting the

---

[9]Van Til, *A Christian Theory of Knowledge*, p. 294; *An Introduction to Systematic Theology*, p. 27.

facts. Moreover, direct appeals to evidence could not introduce the nonbeliever to the truth of God. The "facts" that sinners believe are the opposite of God's truth.

An indirect method, on the other hand, takes into view not only facts but the God who created, controls, and interprets the facts. As Van Til assures us, ". . . without the presupposition of the God of Christianity, we cannot even interpret one fact correctly."[10] An indirect appeal to evidences attempts to bring the unbeliever's attention *back to the facts* by confronting him with the *God* of the facts. It acknowledges the self-attesting Christ of Scripture to be our apologetic "starting-point."[11]

But would this mean that we should announce our presuppositions at the start of every apologetic encounter? Is that what Van Til has in mind when he speaks of starting with the Christ of Scripture?

Some have taken him to mean exactly that. Unless presuppositions are declared in the opening sentences of discourse with nonbelievers, some students of Van Til grow uneasy for fear of capitulating to pagan thought. But that is not what Van Til teaches. Of course, his emphasis has always been that we unashamedly submit to the authority of Scriptures; lest we think, however, that all discussions must open with pronouncements to that effect, Van Til qualifies his point:

---

[10]Van Til, *Christian-Theistic Evidences*, p. ii.
[11]Van Til, "My Credo," p. 3. See also *The Defense of the Faith*, pp. 113, 179 for language of "starting" or "beginning" with God.

> . . . this does not imply that we must always and in
> every instance bring in the discussion of authority at the
> outset of every argument with those we seek to win for
> Christianity. This may frequently be omitted, if only we
> ourselves do not fall into the temptation of thinking
> that we can stand on neutral ground with those who
> hold to a non-Christian position.[12]

Here Van Til indicates that our one and only *episte-mological* starting-point must be kept intact, though there are any number of *topical* starting-points which may be discussed before explicit mention is made of God's authority.[13] It seems, then, that there are two senses in which we may begin or start an apologetic discussion. The one is a logical or epistemological starting-point, having to do with the ultimate point of reference for knowledge. The other is a temporal starting-point, having to do with the sequence in which we choose to discuss various topics.

Given that distinction, it is proper to start with any fact whatsoever when talking with non-Christians. The discussion need not proceed in a logical progression from the most ultimate Christian commitments to those of lesser centrality. We need not hold back the evidences until all our presuppositions are on the table. The quotation by Van Til, above, would lead us to think that there are other ways to be true to biblical authority, ways in which we can be uncompromising presupposi-

---

[12]Van Til, *Christian-Theistic Evidences*, p. 54.

[13]In Van Til's terms, all facts provide a "proximate" or "immediate starting point," i.e., *metaphysical* common ground, whereas the "ulti-mate starting point" is that *epistemological* ground not shared with non-Christians (*Survey of Christian Epistemology*, pp. 120, 130, 204).

tionalists even when we begin our discussion with evidences.

For Van Til, "All knowledge is inter-related."[14] And "if one knows 'nature' truly, one also knows nature's God truly."[15] This is another way of saying that nature, when properly understood, provides a perspective on the whole system of Christian theism. According to Van Til, to know one thing truly, one must know all things truly.[16]

The point is not that Van Til requires us to be omniscient. It is rather that knowledge of one fact in relation to God's ultimate authority entails *implications* for all facts, since they, too, must come under that same authority. Thus, by what Van Til labelled "the method of implication," the Christian can know something about everything, at least in the broadest outline.[17]

Take, for example, the fact of Christ's resurrection. One cannot truly understand the resurrection of Jesus without also knowing something about such other doctrines as the sonship of Jesus and the creation of the universe. The fact of the resurrection calls into view other doctrines of the faith and thus—in a reduced form—the whole system.

As I have noted before, Frame has called this approach "perspectivalism." He points out that, for Van Til, ". . . there are relations of dependence among biblical doctrines."[18] Any one of several major doctrines could

---

[14]Van Til, *An Introduction to Systematic Theology*, p. 26.
[15]Ibid.
[16]Ibid.
[17]Van Til, *Survey of Christian Epistemology*, pp. 6–7.
[18]Frame, *Van Til: The Theologian*, p. 10.

be considered more or less central to the whole system. And if one central teaching is denied, the whole system is denied. For example, the doctrine of the atonement requires a certain doctrine of God, of man, and of sin. Frame notes also that each of the Ten Commandments offers a perspective on all sin and obedience: to disobey one commandment is to violate in principle each of the rest.[19]

Another example of perspectivalism involves the fruit of the Spirit. The "fruit" mentioned in Galatians 5:22 is singular, yet it entails a long list of virtues each of which characterizes spirituality. If you have the fruit of the Spirit at all, you will manifest all the virtues to varying degrees. It would be inconceivable to have the fruit of the Spirit and yet be completely lacking in patience or faithfulness or the other forms of spiritual fruit.

It is enlightening to notice the various perspectives on the gospel throughout Scripture. In John 5:24 eternal life is promised to all who believe in Jesus' Word and in the Father who sent Him. Luke 4:18, 19 focuses on the gospel to the poor, including release to captives, sight to the blind, and freedom to the downtrodden. Paul proclaimed to the Corinthians "nothing . . . except Jesus Christ, and Him crucified" (I Cor. 2:2). The rich young ruler was ordered by Jesus, ". . . go and sell your possessions and give to the poor, and you shall have treasure in heaven; and come, follow me" (Matt. 19:21). And in James 1:27, pure and undefiled religion is "to visit

---

[19]Ibid., p. 13.

orphans and widows in their distress and to keep oneself unstained by the world."[20]

The most explicit and complete gospel summary, of course, is I Corinthians 15:1, 3-4 where Paul announces, "Now I make known to you brethren, the gospel which I preached to you . . . that Christ died for our sins according to the Scriptures, and that He was buried, and that He was raised on the third day according to the Scriptures. . . ." Yet all the above passages somehow summarize the gospel, at least implicitly, though they do not say precisely the same things. Each reduces the gospel according to a particular emphasis, often suited to a given context. But none of these reductions is meant to exclude the others. When the key terms of each are explicated, all the passages convey the same message. Inasmuch as each focuses on some aspect or aspects of the whole gospel, each implies the rest.[21]

This slight digression is meant to illustrate the perspectival relationship between particular beliefs within

---

[20]Several of these and the following examples were first suggested in an interesting study on gospel reductions, written by a friend and former classmate, Steve Larson. He submitted the paper in a course concerning the "contextualization" of theology for missionary purposes. See also Micah 6:8, "And what does the Lord require of you but to do justice, to love kindness, and to walk humbly with your God?"; Matt. 18:3, "Truly I say to you, unless you are converted and become like children, you shall not enter the kingdom of heaven." Also, Matt. 7:7; 10:39; 11:29; 22:34-40; 25:34-40.

[21]I am using Vern Poythress's distinction between an "emphasizing reduction," which may be a legitimate perspectival focus or emphasis, and an "exclusive reductionism," which wrongly absolutizes one perspective to the exclusion of others; *Philosophy, Science, and the Sovereignty of God* (Philadelphia: Presbyterian and Reformed Publishing Co., 1976), pp. 48-49.

Christianity and the system as a whole. The pattern of interdependence holds true not only for the major doctrines of systematic theology, but, as Van Til seems to say, for each and every fact: ". . . the whole claim of Christian theism is in question *in any debate about any fact*."[22]

So, the Christian apologist may begin with any fact because, no matter what facts he wishes to discuss, the stakes are ultimately the same. In every case, Christian theism is in question. Do the facts belong to God or do they not? The challenge for the apologist is to treat the facts in a way that calls the God of Scripture—including the Christian system—into view.

That may sound like an impossible undertaking. How can the whole theistic system be brought to expression in any one discussion of facts? It could take hours, weeks, years, a lifetime to place the whole system of truth before the nonbeliever. Besides the time difficulty, the apologist would have to be a genius to present the total picture—and the non-Christian, a tenacious listener to take it all in. Moreover, you would have to spend nearly all of your time piecing together the theological framework and would never get around to introducing other evidences. Is this what Van Til wants? Are we back to devoting ourselves almost exclusively to presuppositions with virtually no appeal to evidences?

Van Til must have anticipated that question. His explanation comes right to the point:

---

[22]Van Til, *Apologetics*, p. 73, my emphasis.

> This does not imply that it will be possible to bring the whole debate about Christian theism to full expression in every discussion of individual historical fact. . . . It means that no Christian apologist can afford to forget the claim of his system with respect to any particular fact.[23]

Whether we are able to bring Christian theism to a more full expression or only to a partial one, the goal is to express the biblical system through the facts. Van Til explains that when the apologist presents his philosophy of fact with his facts, "he does not need to handle less facts in doing so."[24] The point is that facts should serve as "manifestations" of the Christian system.[25] The extent to which the system can be unfolded in a particular discussion of facts depends on several variables, including the time available, the relative centrality of facts under consideration, and the tolerance of the nonbeliever. But what is important is that any fact can be the topical starting-point for an apologetic confrontation.

One way to depict this principle is to say that the Christian *never has to "change the subject"* in order to do apologetics. He may start with any fact he and his nonbelieving companion happen to be discussing. No matter where they begin the conversation, they are on God's property—the facts are His; they all have implications for Christian theism. And if one understands any fact, he understands that Jesus is Lord over the facts.

---

[23]Ibid., p. 75; *The Defense of the Faith*, p. 118.
[24]Van Til, *A Christian Theory of Knowledge*, p. 298.
[25]Van Til, *Apologetics*, p. 75.

Yet there is another sense in which the apologist *always has to "change the subject."* He must always change the subject because he is concerned to express *God's* facts rather than some fictitious system of "facts." He must always tell sinners that the state of affairs is much different from what they imagine. Unless the apologist changes the subject in this sense, he will never get around to portraying the Christian system. And without that, he will not do justice to any of the facts he endeavors to discuss.

How does one "change the subject" in the sense necessary? How does one show non-Christians the difference between the truth and lies, especially when these nonbelievers often utter the same truths we do and on the whole use the same language we do to describe the world? How do we tell sinners that they are mistaken not only in "religious" matters but in regard to atoms and apples and armadillos and automobiles?

The answer lies in this Van Tilian principle: ". . . the Christian doctrine of God implies a definite concept of everything in the created universe."[26] This principle, coupled with a reminder that sinners and believers share no common concepts on which to build, leads to the following conclusion: The task of the Christian apologist is largely one of redefining the terms of our experience. Those terms may concern such ultimate notions as "God," "truth," "good," "right," "justice," "life," and "man"; or they may be the language in which we describe the mundane facts of our experience when we

---

[26]Van Til, *The Defense of the Faith*, p. 12.

say, "It rained in Philadelphia last night" or "Apples grow on trees" or "My car window is broken." Rain and apples and car windows provide a more tangible, evidential point of departure but may and should lead to a discussion of deeper concepts as the occasion allows. A redefinition of rain or apples or broken windows will eventually lead back to a redefinition of God, not according to the nonbeliever's categories, but according to scriptural categories.

A sample dialogue is taken from an actual conversation I had with a nonbeliever:

non-Christian: My car window is broken!

Christian: Things like that happen in a sinful world.

non-Christian: You mean God is punishing me by breaking my window?

Christian: The truth is, all sorts of things go wrong because man refuses to live God's way.

non-Christian: Well, the way I look at it, my car window is proof that God does not exist: a good God would not permit my window to be broken.

Christian: I agree with you on one point: the god you are talking about *does not* exist. There is no god who protects all car windows unconditionally. But I'm not defending *that* concept of God. I'm talking about someone else—a God who allows windows to be broken for a reason, One who is good in all His ways, who opposes evil and yet forgives men who turn from their sin to follow

Christ. You haven't even considered *this* kind of God. If you had, it would mean that your view of "good," too, would have changed, as well as your outlook on what God has to say about the consequences of sin.

This dialogue, of course, is condensed. Much more could be added, some of which we shall consider as we go on. The movement from the fact to the expression of certain Christian commitments is not always so rapid. But the process of "changing the subject" is shown here. And the point is that nonbelievers would rather not entertain the *biblical* concept of God or the *biblical* notion of good or, for that matter, any item or fact biblically understood. To do so is to accommodate an authority structure that requires a new outlook on all the facts. The world of experience becomes a new creation. All things become new so that even our definitions must undergo regeneration at their root level. In principle, all facts portray experience in terms which *by definition* prove Christian theism.[27]

Viewing the apologetic task as a conflict of definitions and categories is not foreign to Van Til's thought. As long as the apologist remains faithful to the scriptural message, he may even use language coined by the non-

---

[27]Van Til explained in *Survey of Christian Epistemology*, pp. 206-7, "If one really saw that it is necessary to have God in order to understand the grass that grows outside his window, he would certainly come to a saving knowledge of Christ, and to the knowledge of the absolute authority of the Bible. . . . the investigation of any fact whatsoever will involve a discussion of the meaning of Christianity as well as of theism, and a sound position taken on the one involves a sound position taken on the other."

believing philosophical community: "Is not the important thing that Christian meanings be contrasted with non-Christian meanings?" asks Van Til.[28] When this is done in a discussion beginning with any fact, the apologist is able to "remind" the sinner of the God-given significance which the facts rightfully carry.

Facts or evidences handled in this fashion become the *occasion* or *vehicle* on which the Christian system may be introduced. This use of evidences is not at all a substitute for presuppositional inquiry. In the actual discussion of evidences, presuppositions are brought to the foreground increasingly as the dialogue progresses. Hence, presuppositions gain expression through evidences. And evidences derive their meaning from presuppositions. Their relationship is a circle of interdependence.

Van Til makes this point when he talks about general and special revelation: ". . . revelation in nature and revelation in Scripture are mutually meaningless without one another and mutually fruitful when taken together."[29] Jointly they form "God's one grand scheme of covenant revelation of himself to man."[30] Both general and special revelation possess divine authority.[31] But Scripture, as "the finished product of God's supernatural and saving revelation to man" carries final authority extending over all of nature.[32] After all, Scripture is authoritative in all matters to which it speaks,

---

[28]Van Til, *The Defense of the Faith*, p. 23.
[29]Van Til, "Nature and Scripture," p. 269.
[30]Ibid., p. 267.
[31]Ibid., p. 272f.
[32]Van Til, *Apologetics*, p. 36.

and it speaks directly or indirectly to all matters, including all the facts of nature.[33] Thus all evidences in the natural world not only bear authority as general revelation—they convey the authority of Scripture itself via its interpretation of the facts. In other words, since the inscripturation of God's Word, the facts belong to Scripture. That is what makes them *evidences*. "Facts" possess genuine evidential import and impact *to the extent that they present Scripture.*

In his endorsement of a type of theistic proofs, Van Til explained, "They are but the restatement of the revelation of God. . . ."[34] For the same reason, *evidences* may be described as the "restatement" of Scripture. *Christian evidences say what the Scriptures say.* Otherwise they are not evidences at all.

Like Van Til, Frame teaches that facts express the meaning or application of Scripture. For example, the biblical doctrine of Jesus' resurrection *means* that the tomb was empty, that the risen Jesus was seen by many,[35] that the apostles were transformed, and many other observable facts. Those evidences mean what the Scriptures say. With that pattern in mind, Frame describes evidences and biblical presuppositions as two perspectives on the same body of truth. Fundamentally, he notes, "Presuppositions and evidences are one."[36]

---

[33]Ibid., p. 2; *The Defense of the Faith*, p. 8.

[34]Van Til, *Common Grace and the Gospel*, p. 181.

[35]Paul goes to some length to list the many appearances of the resurrected Lord in I Corinthians 15. It is of interest that even the appearances seem to come under the heading of "the gospel which I preached to you" (v. 1).

[36]Frame, "Doctrine of the Knowledge of God" (lecture outline, 1976), p. 10.

But how does a fact, such as that someone's car window is broken, serve as a restatement of Scripture? What biblical truths are signified by that event?

Among other things, the broken window bears out the biblical teaching that material possessions are not permanent—"treasures on earth" do not last (Matt. 6:19). Moreover, it serves as application of the principle that the world is abnormal, having been "subjected to futility" due to sin (Rom. 8:20). At the same time, the incident speaks of God's restraint upon the destructive effects of sin: the window may have been broken but the whole car was not demolished. Had God not issued a promise of redemption along with the curse following Adam's sin, destruction would have been immediate and total (Rom. 8:20ff.; Gen. 2:17; 3:15ff.).

Other principles speak of the need for a godly response to hardships. As upsetting as a broken window may be, it is not a great loss in comparison to the concerns of God's kingdom—life does not consist in earthly possessions (Luke 12:15ff.). Ultimately it is the Lord who gives and who takes away (Job 1:21). After all, He created and owns all things (Gen. 1:1; Ps. 24:1, 2). And for those who love that sovereign Creator, such inconveniences actually work together for the best results (Rom. 8:28; James 1:2ff.). Fundamentally, the fact of the broken window represents a challenge or demand to love Christ more than material things—"No one can serve two masters. . . . You cannot serve God and Mammon" (Matt. 6:24).

It may seem farfetched to call these principles into a simple conversation over a broken window. I do not suggest that they need be brought in all at once. It would take quite some time to develop these ideas clearly in any conversation. But when a Christian looks at something like a broken car window, these are the principles which ought to shape his understanding. And to whatever extent he is able to discuss the incident with a nonbeliever, those and other biblical principles should begin to receive expression.

If it is legitimate at all to say that God teaches us through troublesome experiences, that is the same as saying that such experiences evidence God's truth. Not that they provide revelation independent of Scripture— all the norms for interpreting our experience are to be found in the Bible. But when biblical light is cast on events in our lives, as indeed all men are required to walk in the light, our experiences—even troublesome ones—are used by God to tell us something.

In the example above, a broken window exemplifies what the Bible talks about in the verses cited. It becomes more than a brute fact about shattered glass. It becomes a reminder of God's providence, man's fallenness, Jesus' lordship. The doctrines of creation, the fall, and redemption plus all of their corollaries are linked to a proper understanding of this one fact. To see the fact for what it signifies is to recognize it as evidence for the truth of God's Word.

When a fact is interpreted according to the norms of Scripture, that fact becomes an expression of Scripture's authority. That is how evidences participate in the Bible's self-attestation. Christian evidences are the occasion for Scripture's claim on its own behalf. By invoking the Bible's interpretation they confront men with the self-attesting Christ of Scripture. His authority is brought before sinners, thereby challenging them to forsake their pretense of autonomy and acknowledge Jesus as Lord.

Dr. Van Til characterizes the presentation of evidences as a "reminding process" because evidences lay before nonbelievers just the sort of thing they wish to forget: that Jesus is Lord; that the facts belong to God; that covenantal obligations are writ large on every fact; and that nonbelievers harbor a spirit of rebellion, which prohibits them from recognizing the facts for what they are. That is why Van Til stresses, "Apologetics [including evidences] . . . is valuable to the precise extent that it presses the truth upon the attention of the natural man."[37]

The sinner desperately needs to know where he stands before God. Thus, "It is part of the task of Christian apologetics to make men self-consciously either covenant keepers or covenant breakers."[38] Unless we direct the nonbeliever's attention to the facts as they are portrayed by Scripture, he will not have reason to suspect his blindness to the truth or his need for Christ.

Christian evidences are able to rise to the occasion. Since they depict the state of affairs according to Scripture, they "tell it like it is." As presuppositional evidences, they call all men to acknowledge the Triune God, the final reference point for all meaning and truth. They are, in the truest sense of the term, "Christian-theistic" evidences.

---

[37]Van Til, *The Defense of the Faith*, pp. 104–5.
[38]Van Til, *Apologetics*, p. 27.

8
Objections
and Replies

A look at the more common objections raised against Van Til's presuppositionalism, along with replies, should help gather in some of the loose ends that have survived my efforts to be systematic so far. If that aim is achieved, this chapter will better clarify what Van Til does and does not maintain concerning the relationship of presuppositions to evidences.

Van Til stresses the need for "starting with God." In the previous chapter I discussed two senses of "starting with god" that are not always distinguished by Van Til's followers. The issue is raised again in this chapter, this time by his critics—all the objections presented here revolve around this problematic notion of one's apologetic "starting-point." It is of interest to us to see how Van Til's rivals interpret him on this issue, and to compare those interpretations with what Van Til would say in reply.

We will look at the criticisms first. Probably the most severe complaint comes from Clark Pinnock's essay,

"The Philosophy of Christian Evidences" (although it is difficult to outdo Montgomery's "Once Upon an A Priori" for sheer wit). First, Dr. Pinnock accuses Van Til of beginning with "the axiom that God exists and the Bible is true, to which all the other Christian beliefs are deductively appended."[1] Apparently, Pinnock regards the Van Tilian presupposition of God's existence to be a *pre*-supposition, in the sense that one believes it *before* examining the truthfulness of Christianity. So Pinnock adds, "The basis of the choice cannot be known until after the axiom has been espoused." This grievance gives rise to the charge that Van Til's starting-point is "voluntaristic," "an existential leap of faith."[2] Then, Pinnock likens Van Til's apologetic to "a form of irrational fideism."[3] Gordon Lewis concurs: "It often sounds as though Van Til voluntarily presupposes the truth of Christian claims in a vacuum."[4] Lewis adds that Van Til "short-circuits the apologetic question."[5]

The list of indictments continues with Dr. Van Til ignoring Scripture: Van Til "works from a logical construction to Christ and the gospel," declares Pinnock, "rather than starting with actual revelation." And again, Van Til "has made the objective data of divine revelation inaccessible to the non-Christian. . . ."[6] Hence,

---

[1]Pinnock, "The Philosophy of Christian Evidences," p. 422.

[2]Ibid., p. 423.

[3]Ibid., p. 425.

[4]Lewis, "Van Til and Carnell," p. 351.

[5]Gordon R. Lewis, *Testing Christianity's Truth Claims, Approaches to Christian Apologetics* (Chicago: Moody Press, 1976), p. 287.

[6]Pinnock, "The Philosophy of Christian Evidences," p. 422.

he has "disregarded [the Bible's] contents in his episte-mology."[7] Pinnock alleges that Van Til holds a coher-ence theory of truth, rather than a correspondence view which accounts for the facts.[8]

"Theology-in-a-circle . . . has no compelling rele-vance to the world . . . ," surmises Pinnock in another context.[9] And Dr. Montgomery contests that presup-positionalism does not really challenge the assumptions of nonbelievers: ". . . the irresistible force meets the immovable object . . . ," and neither believer nor non-believer is willing to budge.[10] Montgomery goes so far as to say that Van Til's presuppositionalism gives the non-Christian "excuse" for disbelief by withholding the facts upon which a decision for Christ can be made.[11]

Others have raised similar objections against Van Til. The criticisms mentioned here should give ample oppor-tunity to shed added light on presuppositionalism and its use of evidences.

The following replies are not necessarily Van Til's own responses directed explicitly to the charges cited. In most cases, I am reconstructing replies by drawing from his writings, many of which have been cited already. Some other supporting references will be sup-plied as we go along. In either case, my aim is to repre-

---

[7]Ibid., p. 421.
[8]Ibid.
[9]Pinnock, *Set Forth Your Case*, p. 6.
[10]Montgomery, "Once Upon an A Priori," p. 387.
[11]Ibid., p. 389.

sent faithfully Van Til's position in response to the accusations raised.

Clark Pinnock's appraisal of Van Til remains as disturbing today as it was in 1971 when it first appeared in *Jerusalem and Athens*, the *Festschrift* for Dr. Van Til celebrating his seventy-fifth birthday. Many of the charges raised by Pinnock had actually been denied by Van Til long *before* that volume was composed. For example, Van Til had held all along that Christian doctrines "are not to be obtained by way of deduction from some master concept."[12] Although this statement predated the first accusation listed above, it would be hard to imagine a more pointed negation of the charge. Then, too, Van Til had always made the point that "Christianity is not irrational" and that "it must not be taken on blind faith."[13]

Never does Van Til urge belief in God *before* considering the reasons or evidence for belief. The conditions under which someone believes Christianity are anything but a vacuum, according to Van Til. There is, first of all, the general revelation, which surrounds man with proof of God's existence. Added to this is God's expressed saving revelation, which, as Van Til insists, sinners must hear *in order to believe.*

Far from a blind voluntarism, Van Til stresses acceptance of what is clearly seen and authoritatively attested to. If anything, he calls men to forsake irrational, voluntaristic rebellion—to turn from autonomous exer-

---

[12]Van Til, *The Defense of the Faith*, p. 7.
[13]Van Til, *Common Grace and the Gospel*, p. 184.

tions of the will and vain speculations, and fall submissively into the hands of the revealed Lord.

Neither a principle of coherence nor a principle of correspondence is elevated by Van Til above the Lord's authority. The systematic coherence of Christianity as well as its correspondence to the factual state of affairs are both results of true knowledge being derived from God who is Three in One, and who controls the diverse affairs of the world by His unified plan.

Yes, voluntarism is a problem—a greater one than perhaps Pinnock realizes. For it is he who divorces defense from proclamation, thereby hoping sinners will embrace certain prerequisite beliefs *before* the gospel message is introduced. To be sure, voluntarism is an apologetic heresy. But the guilt does not lie with the method of presuppositionalism—it lies with the method of pre-evangelism. The latter method, not the former, deliberately withholds the scriptural interpretation of reality by making its appeal to brute fact. Since, however, "brute fact" is a contradiction in terms (equaling "meaningless" or "factless fact") such an appeal calls for "faith" of the most blind sort.

On the other hand, Van Til's apologetic stresses epistemological awareness: "To argue by presupposition is to indicate what are the epistemological and metaphysical principles that underlie and control one's method."[14] Here a presupposition is not just one more bias leading to a stalemate between Christians and non-Christians. That would make apologetics a futile enter-

---

[14]Van Til, *The Defense of the Faith*, p. 99.

prise amounting to either a shouting match between insistent opponents or simply a dead silence. Dr. Van Til avoids this kind of hopeless standoff by drawing on the principle that faith comes by hearing—hearing the *Word of Christ*. By the very nature of the case, Christian-theistic presuppositions are the bearers of the gospel message. Unlike formal prejudices, they are the ultimate truths which receive meaningful expression as they interpret the facts of our experience.

Van Til's followers and foes alike should take note: Presuppositionalism is not a matter of intellectual arm-twisting—its effectiveness does not hinge on the dogmatic *disposition* of the apologist or his insistence that he is right and his opponent is wrong. Presupposition-alism is effective to the extent to which the dogma itself is presented. When the Word of truth is proclaimed the Spirit of God accompanies that Word with power to break down rebellion and transform sinful minds.

Far from withholding revelation from sinners, Van Til's apologetic is designed to draw attention to God's Word at every turn. The message and the evidence are presented to provide "a fertile ground for the Holy Spirit. . . ."[15] And Van Til urges that "by stating the argument as clearly as we can, we may be the agents of the Spirit in pressing the claims of God upon men."[16]

So it is difficult to figure out what prompted some of the objections voiced by Pinnock and the others. Admittedly, Van Til's argument is circular. That's because it is

---

[15] Van Til, "My Credo," p. 21.
[16] Van Til, *Common Grace and the Gospel*, p. 62.

systematic. All systematic arguments are ultimately circular—they all rely on a particular system which enables some conclusions and not others. Van Til's point is that the Christian circle of thought can be presented *for what it is,* because *it possesses the power and authority to subdue* what would otherwise be a vicious circle on the part of nonbelievers. If the non-Christian will "place himself upon the Christian position for argument's sake . . . ,"[17] he will be confronted with God's authoritative interpretation of the evidences, which is to say he will be confronted with the authoritative Lord. No other challenge or offense is necessary.

The criticisms issued by Pinnock result largely from a faulty distinction between presuppositions and evidences. He seems to say that one may *either* argue by presupposition *or* appeal to historical facts.[18] With that dilemma in mind, Pinnock naturally endorses the hard facts. For him, it is a question of whether one offers the message or not. Obviously, Christians ought to present the facts of the gospel. What could be wrong with that?

The problem is that Dr. Pinnock overlooks the intricate interplay between presuppositions and facts. Both he and Dr. Montgomery seem unaware that they, as believers, are sitting on a gold-mine of presuppositions. In the past they have dipped into that hidden treasure most noticeably when confronted with the question of biblical inerrancy, yet without admitting the cash-value of the presuppositional method. Until recently it was

---

[17]Van Til, *The Defense of the Faith,* p. 100.
[18]Pinnock, "The Philosophy of Christian Evidences," p. 421.

Pinnock who would say, "Infallibility is a necessary inference to be drawn from the biblical doctrine of inspiration";[19] or else, "Scripture nowhere suggests a canon outside itself by which it is to be judged";[20] and again, "Inductive difficulties encountered in the text cannot change the fact that the Bible claims not to err."[21]

Language like this does not do much to confute Van Til's position. Indeed, Christian apologists who oppose his stance have unadmittedly made it their posture now and then when pressed under the weight of certain issues. Biblical inerrancy is that kind of issue.

It is sad to note, however, that in recent years Dr. Pinnock has bowed in the direction of inerrancy's opponents. Somehow since his admirable *Defense of Biblical Infallibility* (1967) he has decided that the "inductive difficulties" *do* undermine the Bible's claim not to err. In a volume entitled *Biblical Authority* (1977) both Pinnock and Ramm join Jack Rogers (ed.), Paul Rees, Berkeley Mickelsen, Earl Palmer, and David Hubbard in their tribute to a *fallible* Bible.[22] "Of course the Bible is error-ridden," Pinnock announces at one point.[23] And from there he applauds Barth, a "powerful

---

[19]Pinnock, "Our Source of Authority: the Bible," *Bibliotheca Sacra*, 124, No. 494 (April–June, 1967), 154. See also *A Defense of Biblical Infallibility* (Philadelphia: Presbyterian and Reformed Publishing Co., 1967), p. 10.

[20]Pinnock, *A Defense of Biblical Infallibility*, p. 8.

[21]Ibid., p. 18.

[22]Jack Rogers, ed., *Biblical Authority* (Waco, TX: Word Books, 1977).

[23]Pinnock, "Three Views of the Bible in Contemporary Theology," ibid., p. 52.

ally . . . in the defense of biblical authority,"[24] whose critical honesty Pinnock finds preferable to the "Warfieldian theory of perfect errorlessness."[25]

It is startling to see where an inductive method will take you as it casts judgment on the trustworthiness of scriptural phenomena independently of biblical presuppositions. The irony is that while Warfield favored that inductive method, others have followed it precisely to a denial of his strong inerrancy position. Daniel Fuller, for one, buttressed his limited inerrancy view by making frequent appeals to Warfield.[26]

But the crucial difference between Warfield and a Fuller, a Pinnock, or a Ramm is that Warfield, though not an avowed presuppositionalist, remained fundamentally committed to the Bible's claim not to err. He spoke, for instance, in favor of an "immense presumption against alleged facts contradictory of the biblical doctrine."[27] It is not that Warfield's "presumption" for Christianity represented a presupposition in the Van Tilian sense. Warfield's presumption did not boast absolute certainty. Yet one has to wonder: would Warfield or, today, Montgomery ever really allow particular evidences to count against the claims of Scripture? It is hard to imagine that either would.

---

[24]Ibid., p. 56.

[25]Ibid., p. 68.

[26]Daniel Fuller, "The Nature of Biblical Inerrancy," *Journal of the American Scientific Affiliation*, 24, No. 2 (June, 1972), 47–51. See also Dewey Beegle, *The Inspiration of Scripture* (Philadelphia: Westminster Press, 1963).

[27]Warfield, "The Real Problem of Inspiration," p. 214.

Even Pinnock would deny that the *claims* of Scripture contain error. For although he takes issue with War-fieldian inerrancy, he is happy with the Lausanne Covenant position that Scripture is "without error in all that it *affirms*."[28] So even Pinnock, the opponent of presuppositionalism, and now the opponent of absolute inerrancy, is held partially in check by remnant biblical presuppositions.

My point is that all Christian apologists presuppose certain biblical commitments, regardless of whether they are willing to *call* them presuppositions. The wide discrepancy between Christian apologists arises from the varying degrees of consistency with which they honor those commitments in their apologetic method.

Van Til has adopted the best principles of Warfield and Kuyper and has developed an apologetic which is amazingly consistent with Scripture. In doing so, he has ignored neither Scripture nor the facts of experience. He freely invites nonbelievers to search both the Scriptures and the laboratory in order to see the facts for what they are.[29] His presuppositions are anything but empty postulates—they make full use of Christian evidences, the interpretation of which is the proclamation of God's Word.

---

[28]Pinnock, "Three Views of the Bible," p. 68, my emphasis. How then does Pinnock differ from Warfield? Do not they both hold that the Bible is free of error in all it *intends* to say? Clearly the controversy is over what the Bible does and does not intend to affirm in each context. That being the question, there is no warrant for claiming the Scriptures contain *errors*, especially since Scripture unmistakably intends to say it is *God's* Word.

[29]Van Til, *Apologetics*, p. 2.

PART IV
Biblical Examples
and Summary

9

Resurrection Evidences
at Work

ONLY a few illustrations of the use of evidences
have been offered until now. This chapter should
help to make up for that lack by examining
several biblical examples. The examples are found in
passages which depict, in a variety of ways, the use of
evidences pertaining to the resurrection of Jesus. My
purpose is to show not only how evidences can be and
have been employed, but also how Van Til's apologetic
admirably accounts for the type of treatment evidences
receive in these texts.

Five passages will be considered: one from John's
Gospel, three from the book of Acts, and one from
Paul's first letter to the Corinthians.

John 20:24-29

John describes Jesus' post-resurrection appearance to
Thomas. In this setting, Jesus is the apologist, and

Thomas, the disbeliever.[1] The other disciples had already reported to him that they had seen the risen Christ. But Thomas would not believe. In effect, he set up his very own verification criterion: he demanded visual and tangible evidence that Jesus was raised. Thomas would believe only if Christ could pass the empirical test.

When Jesus appeared before the doubter, there was no shortage of physical evidence. The correspondence between Thomas's demands in verse 25 and Jesus' fulfillment in verse 27 is noteworthy:

Thomas	Jesus
Unless I shall see in His hands the imprint of the nails,	see My hands;
and put my finger into the place of the nails,	reach here your fingers;
and put my hand into His side,	reach here your hand, and put it into My side;
I will not believe.	and be not unbelieving, but believing.

Yet there is more going on here than simply a physical display. Thomas's response makes that clear: "My Lord and my God!" (v. 28).[2]

---

[1]In a very real sense Jesus is always *the* apologist—*we* do not confront sinners. Whenever we do apologetics we draw men's attention to the claims of the authoritative Lord.

[2]Leon Morris notes that until this incident, no one had addressed Jesus in such exalted terms. *The Gospel According to John* (Grand Rapids, Mich: Wm. B. Eerdmans, 1975), pp. 853–54.

Why did not Thomas answer in a well-what-do-you-know manner? Why was he not simply amused, intrigued, perplexed, suspicious? The answer is that he had been confronted with the Lord. The evidence Thomas observed not only showed him the hands and side of Jesus: the evidence signified the authority of the risen Lord and God. This was no brute appearance. The divine character of Jesus was expressed in several ways. He had miraculously entered the room even though the doors were locked (v. 26). His very first words were, "Peace be with you" (v. 26), indicating that this was the same Jesus who had promised peace and who had "overcome the world."[3] He had demonstrated omniscience as well as condescending patience in matching the demands of Thomas point by point. In humility He showed the wounds that would atone for sin. And with all this His authority was accented by His command to believe.

Thus, the value of all the evidence was its significance within a particular framework of understanding. In the passage there is a pronounced shift away from the physical wounds themselves to the self-attesting Christ who "was pierced through for our transgressions" and "crushed for our iniquities" (Isa. 53:5). The evidence was more than enough, and there is no indication in the text that Thomas ever followed through with his empirical test. Suddenly that had become unnecessary. The

---

[3] John 14:27, "Peace I leave with you, My peace I give to you, not as the world gives, do I give to you. Let not your heart be troubled, nor let it be fearful." John 16:33, "These things I have spoken to you, that in Me you may have peace. In the world you have tribulation, but take courage, I have overcome the world."

tables had been turned, and now it was time for Thomas to answer to the highest authority.

The problem had not been a lack of evidence. In fact, Jesus implied that Thomas should have believed when the disciples first reported the resurrection to him. The problem had been that he had not appreciated their report in light of Jesus' divine authority and His many earlier claims that He would return from the grave.[4] Had Thomas done so, he would never have thought it necessary to call for more evidence. Thus Jesus' words, "Blessed are they who did not see, and yet believed" (v. 29).

Acts 1:3

Like the previous example, this verse depicts Jesus in the role of an apologist. His audience is the apostles whose initial response to His resurrection was disbelief.[5] Here Luke reports that Jesus "presented Himself alive" to the apostles "by many convincing proofs."

The word "proofs" is not too strong a translation of τεκμηρίοις. Calvin saw fit to translate it as such, in contrast to Erasmus who favored "arguments." "Convincing proofs" (NASB and NIV) or "infallible proofs" (KJV) is most proper. The Greek noun τεκμήριον "is used by Plato and Aristotle to denote the strongest proof

---

[4]See Matthew 12:38-40; 16:21; 17:23; 20:19; 27:63; Mark 14:58, plus their parallels.

[5]Mark 16:11; Luke 24:11.

of which a subject is susceptible," writes J. A. Alexander, in his commentary on Acts.[6]

The *form* of the proof is of interest to us. Jesus "presented Himself alive, after His suffering, by many convincing proofs, *appearing* to [the apostles] over a period of forty days, and *speaking* of the things concerning the kingdom of God."

Again the physical appearance of Jesus is placed into meaningful perspective. The proof took the dual form of appearing and speaking, the latter (presuppositions) providing interpretation for the former (evidences). More specifically, Jesus taught His apostles about the kingdom of God, and thereby introduced Himself as King. His kingdom would be characterized by spiritual power (1:5-8). As risen Lord, all power and authority had been granted to Him by the Father; Jesus would therefore send His Spirit with power and abide with His disciples, "even to the end of the age" (Matt. 28:18-20; Cf. John 14:26; 15:26; 20:22; Acts 2:33).

So, Jesus not only "presented Himself *alive*." That in itself would have been interesting, perhaps. But He "presented *Himself* alive"—His speech gave sense to that strange event. As Van Til would say, it was not the mere fact *that* a corpse was resuscitated—the *that* and the *what* combine to make a momentous resurrection attested to by irrefutable proof.

---

[6]Joseph Addison Alexander, *Commentary on the Acts of the Apostles* (Grand Rapids, Mich.: Zondervan, 1956), p. 5.

Acts 2:14-36

This passage helps to illustrate the close interaction of presuppositions with evidences. Here Peter is addressing a crowd of incredulous Jews on the day of Pentecost. The Holy Spirit had been poured out upon the Christians gathered together. When Jews "from every nation" (v. 5) heard their own languages spoken by this band of Galilean Christians, they were bewildered. Yet some resorted to mockery, attributing this manifestation of spiritual power to the intoxicating effect of wine.

Peter's sermon is, therefore, aimed at setting straight this faulty interpretation of the tongues phenomenon. He begins by denying the charge of drunkenness. What the Jews were seeing should be understood as the fulfillment of Joel's prophecy (Joel 2:28-32) that in the last days God's Spirit would be poured out upon all mankind, producing prophecies, visions, dreams, and wonders. The climax of Joel's prophecy is cited by Peter in verse 21: "And it shall be; that every one who calls on the name of the Lord shall be saved."

If the Jews did not understand the significance of the tongues at Pentecost, it was because they did not understand that Jesus is Lord. Peter thus develops an argument for the lordship of Jesus.

The tone of address to the Jews makes it clear that they bear an immense responsibility for their ignorance. Twice Peter emphatically demands their attention implying that his message ought to have special significance for them.[7] He introduces Jesus as "a man attested to you

---

[7] Acts 2:14, "Men of Judea, and all you who live in Jerusalem, let this

by God with miracles and wonders and signs which God performed through Him in your midst, just as you yourselves know" (v. 22). Peter then indicts them for nailing Jesus to a cross "by the hands of godless men" (v. 23).

From the guilt of the Jews, Peter turns quickly to the major point in his argument for Jesus' lordship: "And God raised Him up again, putting an end to the agony of death, since it was impossible for Him to be held in its power" (v. 24).[8] The resurrection of Jesus gives evidence that He is Lord. Peter elaborates by citing David's statement that God would not allow His Holy One to undergo decay or to be abandoned in Hades (v. 27).[9] Lest the Jews think that David was merely referring to himself, Peter assures his audience that David "both died and was buried, and his tomb is with us to this day" (v. 29). No, David was not alluding to himself as a resurrected Lord. Instead, "he looked ahead and spoke of the resurrection of the Christ . . ." (v. 31). Thus Peter announces, "This Jesus God raised up again, to which we are all witnesses" (v. 32). The implied conclusion is that Jesus, therefore, is truly Lord.

---

be known to you, and give heed to my words"; Acts 2:22, "Men of Israel, listen to these words. . . ."

[8]Alexander comments, "The verb ($\kappa\rho\alpha\tau\epsilon\hat{\iota}\sigma\theta\alpha\iota$) which in classical Greek denotes conquest or superiority, in the New Testament always means to hold or to be holden fast, either in a literal or figurative sense, but never perhaps without some trace of its original and proper import, as for instance in the case before us, where the sense is that he could not be permanently held fast by death as a captive or conquered enemy" (*Commentary on the Acts of the Apostles*, p. 72).

[9]From Psalm 16:8-11.

Logicians may wonder about the soundness of Peter's argument. His reasoning seems to run as follows:

1) The Messiah/Lord was to be resurrected.
2) Jesus was resurrected.

Therefore Jesus is the Messiah/Lord.

But would that argument commit the same fallacy as the following?:

1) My cat is a mammal.
2) Your dog is a mammal.

Therefore your dog is my cat.

The fallacy involves an "undistributed" middle term. While it is true that my cat and your dog belong to the class of mammals, they are each a very small part of that class and distinct from each other. Therefore, they are not necessarily connected by the middle term, mammal. The only way this syllogism could be strictly valid is if *all* members of the class of mammals were referred to in at least one premise.

Likewise, in order for Peter's argument to be a valid proof of Jesus' lordship, he would have to show that the Messiah's resurrection and Jesus' resurrection were not two distinguishable types.

Peter does just that. Jesus' resurrection is a one-of-a-kind event. His unique victory over death qualified Him to be exalted to the right hand of God and to receive from the Father the promise of the Holy Spirit whose power was displayed that day (v. 33).

Inasmuch as the risen Savior was granted this ultimate authority, His resurrection corresponds with the description found in Psalm 110:1. The Lord would sit at the right hand of the Father until His enemies were made a footstool for His feet (vv. 34, 35). Thus, on the basis of the prophetic description of the Lord's resurrection, and Jesus' fulfillment thereof, Peter's conclusion is inescapable: "Therefore let all the house of Israel know for certain that God has made Him both Lord and Christ—this Jesus whom you crucified" (v. 36).

The interaction between evidences and presuppositions in this passage is intriguing. For example, the diverse tongues are evidence for the lordship of Jesus, given the fact of the resurrection. In turn, the resurrection is recognized as evidence that Jesus is Lord and Christ, given David's prophecies in Psalms 16 and 110. But then, from another perspective, the tongues serve as evidence for the resurrection, given the character of the Lord described in verse 33.

Does the resurrection act as evidence or as presupposition in this text? It seems to do both. Peter treats it as something which is both evident (in some sense, observable) and presupposed (basic to the interpretation of the phenomena). The pattern here lends generous support to Van Til's emphasis upon the Christian system as a unit and his circular method showing the authority of the self-attesting Lord.

Acts 26

Paul's defense before Agrippa is recorded in this chapter. The apostle had been thrown into jail for preaching the resurrection of Jesus. Thus his argument is implicitly a defense of the resurrection, and not primarily a defense of his life.

This case helps to show the distinction between a temporal or topical starting-point and a logical or epistemological one. Paul chooses to "begin" the defense with a discussion of his life prior to his conversion. He was "a Pharisee according to the strictest sect" (v. 5). And much of the chapter is taken up with the events leading to and including his conversion.

Yet, wedged in the midst of this testimony is Paul's observation of the irony that he was standing trial "for the hope of the promise made by God to our fathers" (v. 6). This is followed by a penetrating rhetorical question: "Why is it considered incredible among you people if God does raise the dead?" (v. 8).

What does this question have to do with the broader discussion of Paul's conversion? The answer is that Paul's conversion enabled him to realize the hope of the promise to Israel. And the substance of that hope is the resurrection of Jesus. While Paul speaks at length of his former life and conversion, he states in verses 22 and 23,

> . . . I stand to this day testifying both to small and great, stating nothing but what the Prophets and Moses said was going to take place; that the Christ was to suffer, and that by reason of His resurrection from the dead He should be the first to proclaim light both to the Jewish people and to the Gentiles.

In other words, Paul's transformed life, including his preaching of Jesus, serves as evidence for the resurrection of Christ.

Several factors accompany that evidence thereby making the resurrection a most credible event. Paul seems to have made a concerted effort to place the whole question within the framework of Old Testament promise. In effect he asks, What is so unbelievable about the fulfillment of God's promises? Surely his Jewish audience would not openly deny the hope of Israel expressed by Moses and the prophets, would they?

But Paul presses the question even deeper. Not only is the credibility of the Old Testament fathers at stake. Ultimately the question boils down to whether God is willing and able to raise the dead. Paul seems to be saying that his conversion and his preaching of the resurrection are "incredible" to the Jews because they had not really considered the God of Scripture.

Paul's use of "if" in verse 8 should not disturb us. He is not suggesting that it is uncertain whether God does raise the dead. His use of "if" (ϵi) carries the sense of "given that" or "supposing" or "presupposing."[10] If one presupposes the biblical God, then the idea of a resurrection from the dead is not incredible at all. *Such* a God is the presuppositional reference point according to which all other matters are decided.

So the general pattern of Paul's defense shows his conversion to be evidence for Jesus' resurrection, given or presupposing the God who revealed His promise to Israel through Moses and the prophets. The facts of Paul's conversion supply the topical starting-point for his defense. But ultimately those facts carry their true evidential import in accordance with his epistemological starting-point, namely Jehovah God. Paul's use of

---

[10]See also Acts 4:9; 11:17; 16:15, for uses of ϵi.

"if" brings that God into fresh view. And his appeals to
Old Testament promise help characterize the God who
alone determines what is or is not genuinely credible.

I Corinthians 15

Here Paul highlights the significance of Jesus' resurrection by examining the consequences of denying that
fact. In the opening verses of the chapter the apostle
places the resurrection of Christ—including His appearances to many eye witnesses—under the description of
"the gospel which I preached to you" (v. 1). The gospel
of Christ *means* that Jesus was raised—more specifically
that He was seen by Cephas, the Twelve, a crowd of over
500, James, the apostles, and finally Paul.

The Corinthian church "received" that gospel (v. 1),
so it is ironic that some among them disbelieved the
resurrection of the dead (v. 12). Paul responds by asking,
in effect, how the Corinthians could disassociate the
resurrection from other parts of the Christian message.
He proceeds to show some of the implications of that
doctrine for the Christian system as a whole.

First, ". . . if there is no resurrection of the dead, not
even Christ has been raised" (v. 13). Second, ". . . if
Christ has not been raised, then our preaching is vain,
your faith also is vain" (v. 14), that is, "empty" or
"contentless" ($\kappa\epsilon\nu\grave{o}\nu$). Third, if the resurrection teaching is not true, the apostles are "false witnesses" (v. 15).
Fourth, without Jesus' resurrection, faith is "worth-
less," that is, "powerless" or "without effect" ($\mu\alpha\tau\alpha\acute{\iota}\alpha$)
and believers are still in their sins (v. 17): those who
have died "have perished" (v. 18). Finally, under such

conditions, Christians "are of all men most to be pitied" (v. 19).

Why does Paul devote so much attention to the idea of Christ *not* being raised? Why set forth hypothetical conditions under which the faith would not be true? Does Paul fear that the remains of Jesus' body may someday be discovered and the gospel would be falsified? Can the Scriptures *not* claim final certainty? Is the resurrection doctrine still in doubt and contingent upon yet unknown phenomena?

That is not Paul's concern. By speaking in terms of what may be called the "hypothetical falsifiability" of Christianity, he draws attention to the meaning of Jesus' resurrection. For example, the resurrection means that the Christian faith is not an empty belief; it means that the apostles were not false witnesses; it means that believers are not stranded in sin and that those who have died in Christ have not perished. In other words, by imagining hypothetical conditions under which Christianity would not be true, Paul illustrates what the resurrection does mean and what it does not.

At no point, however, does Paul hint that the Bible is *actually* in danger of ever being falsified. The hypothetical conditions he mentions could not possibly be realized. Thus, immediately after listing the consequences of denying the resurrection, he declares unmistakably that "Christ has been raised from the dead" (v. 20).

Not only is the actual falsifiability of Christianity ruled out, but Paul is unable to conceive fully of its falsification, even hypothetically. What conclusions could anyone affirm were Jesus not raised? Would there be any human knowledge? Adam would have been struck down immediately were there no genuine hope of resurrection. There would be no human race to contemplate such a condition. The hypothesis is ultimately unthinkable. And if Paul were to follow out the *full* consequences of denying the resurrection, nothing could be said.

Yet, in this passage Paul includes in his list of consequences, statements about God (v. 15) and about sin (v. 17) and judgment (v. 18), as if these doctrines would somehow remain intact. This indicates that Paul's mind was captivated by biblical presuppositions all along. His purpose was not to question whether or not Christianity is true. His aim was to declare the Christian gospel by focusing on the significance of the resurrection. That aim is validated unquestionably throughout the remainder of the chapter. Jesus' resurrection and its rich implications could not be more vividly and convincingly expressed than Paul portrays them there.

The five sample passages we have examined should suffice to illustrate several points emphasized by Van Til: (1) that evidences do have a proper use; (2) that the interpretation of evidence is an ethical, spiritual matter; (3) that whenever evidences are used they are to carry a distinctively Christian significance whereby they express the gospel; (4) that all the facts support Christian theism as a unit; (5) that the relationship between facts and presuppositions is a circular, systematic one; and (6) that the purpose of discussing evidences is to confront sinners with the self-attesting Christ of Scripture.

It is quite possible that other inferences could and

should be drawn from these passages. And innumerable other types of evidences could be considered. My aim has been to illustrate at least the above-mentioned points, drawing from one general area of evidences—the resurrection. Such examples represent only a small segment of the vast field of evidence for the Christian faith. The challenge is to harness more and more of that limitless evidential reserve according to the principles Van Til has developed.

10

Summary

I have tried to be true to Dr. Van Til's apologetic—both his explicit claims and what is implied by them concerning evidences. Here is an attempt to view, in one brief setting, "the total picture." An outline format will help to condense what I believe to be a consistent Van Tilian stance on the often misunderstood study and use of Christian evidences. The outline is set in parallel columns so that the sharp contrast between Christian and non-Christian positions is most clearly illustrated:

A. The facts of God's revelation are known by all men.

1. Non-Christians are covenant-breakers in their treatment of the facts.
   a. Non-Christians attempt to know the facts yet forget God.

2. Christians are, in principle, covenant-keepers in their treatment of the facts.[1]
   a. Christians acknowledge that the facts reveal God.

---

[1] I say "in principle" because Christians do not always, in practice, live up to the principles they have committed themselves to. In this

124

b. Non-Christian "knowledge" is characterized by ethical rebellion against God.

c. Non-Christians "know" only in an intellectual sense.

d. Non-Christians treat the facts as "brute" by emptying them of their significance, especially the obligations toward God that the facts require of men.

e. Non-Christians devise a fiction out of the facts.

b. Christian knowledge is attained in ethical submission to the Lord.

c. Christians know with their whole renewed persons.

d. Christians appreciate the significance of the facts as revelation of Christ's lordship.

e. Christians recognize the facts for what God created them to be.

B. The facts constitute evidential proof for Christian theism.

1. Traditional theistic proof does not make proper use of the facts as God's facts.

   a. Traditional proofs imply that man is an autonomous reference point for interpreting the facts.

   b. With the sinner, traditional proofs appeal to "brute facts."

   c. Traditional proofs regard the factual case for Christianity to be only probable.

2. Genuine evidential proof shows the facts all to be God's facts.

   a. Evidences recognize the Triune God as the ultimate reference point for interpreting the facts.

   b. Evidences treat each fact as proof for Christian theism.

   c. Evidences constitute absolutely valid proof for Christianity.

---

life no Christian is fully consistent: a covenant-keeper may at times behave like a covenant-breaker. But if one is a genuine believer, his basic orientation is that of a covenant-keeper and his treatment of facts will show a general pattern of submission to God.

d. In effect, traditional proofs allow sinners excuse by minimizing the perspicuity of natural revelation and by withholding Scripture from the non-Christian.

d. Evidences allow the sinner no excuse for ignorance.

e. In short, traditional proofs compromise all the biblical teachings including the doctrines of God, man, revelation, creation, the fall, and redemption.

e. Evidences depend on and reflect their presuppositional framework which is the whole system of scriptural doctrines.

C. Therefore a Christian use of evidence must be by indirect rather than direct appeal.

1. Direct appeals to evidence present no true defense of the faith.

2. Indirect appeals defend the faith with unshakable proof.

   a. Direct appeals discuss "facts" rather than present Scripture.

   a. Indirect appeals present evidences as the restatement of Scripture.

   b. Direct appeals carry no authoritative interpretation of the evidence.

   b. Indirect appeals convey the authority of the self-attesting Christ of Scripture.

   c. Direct appeals imply that non-Christians are neutral in their interpretation of facts.

   c. Indirect appeals confront the rebellious will of nonbelievers.

   d. Direct appeals attempt to build understanding on common concepts and categories.

   d. Indirect appeals challenge the concepts and categories of sinners.

   e. Direct appeals do not truly present the facts but allow sinners to continue in fantasy.

   e. Indirect appeals present the facts for what they are and thereby call sinners back to the reality of life in Christ.

"Men have not done justice by the facts, by the evidence of God's presence before their eyes," says Van Til, "unless they burst out into praise of him who has made all things."[2] Christian evidences declare God's glory. They implore us to do the same.

---

[2]Van Til, *A Christian Theory of Knowledge,* p. 234.

General Index

Scripture Index

135